Montegue Blister's

STRANGE GAMES

and other odd things to do with your time

To Siân & Issy

Montegue Blister's

STRANGE GAMES

and other odd things to do with your time

Montegue Blister

FRIDAY
BOOKS

The Friday Project
An imprint of HarperCollins*Publishers*
77–85 Fulham Palace Road
Hammersmith, London W6 8JB
www.thefridayproject.co.uk
www.harpercollins.co.uk

First published by The Friday Project in 2009

1

ISBN 978-0-00-732009-7

Designed and typeset by e-Digital Design. Illustrations by Alan Down
Printed and bound in Great Britain by Clays Ltd, St Ives plc

Sustainable reading
www.harpercollins.co.uk/green
FSC + HarperCollins
Your choice makes a difference

FSC is a non-profit international organization established to promote the responsible
management of the world's forests. Products carrying the FSC label are independently
certified to assure consumers that they come from forests that are managed to meet
the social, economic and ecological needs of present or future generations.

Find out more about HarperCollins and the environment at
www.harpercollins.co.uk/green

CONTENTS

Indoor Games 21

Outdoor Games 51

Urban Games 81

Playground Games 131

INTRO

In 1972, whilst walking towards my brother in our unassuming suburban living room, he flicked out his foot cleverly, catching me on my ankle bone. This caused me to momentarily lose my balance, stumble, then come crashing down onto the Axminster carpet – my head narrowly missing the doily-covered arm of our brown Dralon sofa. Walking Trippy, the game, was born. Then, after just a few hours of experimentation, the rules and strategies for this English Gentleman's martial art were in place.

Thirty years later, after a night of reminiscing, I decided it was time that the whole world was made aware of Walking Trippy – and the blog *Strange Games* was born. As the blog grew I received many emails that mentioned other great, almost forgotten games, such as Split the Kipper and Spectacular Deaths, as well as queries such as what is the best game for keeping a party of hyperactive seven-year-olds under control (that would be Underpants Jumping – see page 39, if you are wondering). And now, three years on, I give you *Strange Games*, the book.

The aim of this book is to detail strange games, unusual sports and bizarre festivals; to reclaim the nation's MTVd-, MP3d-, Bluetoothed-enabled youth. Its mission: to crowbar a generation of sofa-sitting lazy bastards off their backsides and send them, eager and smiling, off to the shin-kicking fields of the Cotswolds. If it results in even one headrest-embedded DVD player being ripped out so that the kids in the back of the car can concentrate on Finger Jousting or slamming their knuckles down on each other, its job will be done.

This book also includes party games, but there is no mention of pass the parcel and there are no games where you dress like Britney Spears and freeze when the music stops. Instead, there are games like Bucketheads, Body Surfing, and politically incorrect gems like Slave Market. And in this time where children's parties get ever more expensive (as parents spend small fortunes employing professional entertainers for their little Joshuas and Jemimas and mobile phones become standard fare for party bags), *Strange Games* makes the revolutionary suggestion that maybe all you need to entertain the little terrors is a roll of gaffer tape and a modicum of imagination.

The world of unusual festivals and sports is well covered here, with entries on events from the well-known Cheese Rolling to the obscure, but soon to be Olympic, sport of Watermelon Ski-ing. Fruit and vegetables seem to play a large part in this world: if you are not strapping them to your feet you are throwing them, spitting their seeds, or head-butting them. Of note in this area of oddness are two locales: Finland and Gloucestershire. Both these places can make claim to being capitals of strange games, with Finland being represented by Swamp Soccer, Mobile Phone Throwing, and Wife Carrying (to name but three), and Gloucestershire by Shin Kicking, Cheese Rolling and Woolsack Carrying.

At the back of this book is a calendar detailing various strange events to go and see. Many of these are open to both spectators and new competitors. The chance to become a world champion in life is rare, but the odds greatly increase if you enter the World Worm Charming Festival or the Frozen Pea Throwing Championships.

And as the nation slips unconsiously into a homogeneous mass of couch-dwelling, fast-food guzzling idiots who watch documentaries about obese people that only eat cheese having their lives changed by Scottish poo inspectors, it is time to grab these aforementioned lazy bastards by their melon balls and force them to Toe Wrestle or play Mob Football, or, at the very least, find their nearest field so they can pick up a cow pat and fling it.

If just one person reads this book and decides to start a Dwile Flunking team, I can rest happy and look forward to meeting my maker with the knowledge that I have played my part in making the world a better place. When I close my eyes I have a vision of St Peter opening those pearly gates, smiling as I walk towards him, his hands extended towards me, palms pressed together. I can see his peaceful face now, as I quickly raise one of my hands and slap the back of one of his as hard as I can.

Note: Some of these games are not suitable for children; indeed, some are not even suitable for adults but are included here because they are intriguing, or were played in the past and therefore of historical interest. Any game or sport that involves cruelty to animals is not in any way endorsed.

Montegue Blister, 2009

HAND AND FEET GAMES

The great thing about playing hand and feet games is that you rarely need any other equipment to be able to play them; just roll up your sleeves or remove a sock and you're ready. As the entries below show, these games often appear to be quite violent. Also (with the exception of Toe Wrestling), the majority of these have a long, and sometimes murky, history. Rock, Paper, Scissors (the oldest) was possibly played by cave dwellers but never took off – perhaps due to the 'Rock' throw being so dominant amongst players of the day.

Bloody Knuckles

Bloody Knuckles gives its name to not one, but two, strange and savage games.

Bloody Knuckles 1: The more usual version of Bloody Knuckles is the knuckular (a technical medical term) version of Slapsies. Here, both players each form one hand into a fist and stand opposite each other, arms outstretched and fists touching. It is the aim of one player to lift their fist (no higher than shoulder height) and bring their knuckles down onto the top of their opponent's fist. Obviously, it is the opponent's job to pull their fist away and avoid a painful blow, but they must not make a move until their opponent starts their attempt. Players can either take turns and gain points for each hit or maintain the strike if contact is made. In the old-fashioned version of this game you are not allowed to move your hand to escape, you just leave it there to get hit and then have your turn. Obviously, that was just barbaric.

Bloody Knuckles 2: Here, players sit at a table across from each other. One player then makes their hand into a fist and places it on the table. The other player takes a heavy coin (a £2 coin, for example), puts it flat on the table, then flicks it with as much force as possible at their opponent's knuckles. Play then reverses and it becomes the first player's turn to form a fist. The game continues until blood is drawn or one player submits, or until both realise they are wasting their lives and decide to go and do something more productive instead.

Bloody Knuckles even has its own governing body – the World Bloody Knuckles Association – which promotes the game and organises regular events.

Extreme Rock, Paper, Scissors and variations

Extreme games and sports are played by fit, highly trained participants and usually involve some degree of danger.

Extreme Rock, Paper, Scissors is just a violent variation on the standard game – basically it's an excuse for a physical attack on your opponent.

As in the normal version, each player decides and forms the hand position to represent rock, paper or scissors; however, if paper wins it is translated as a slap and the player who wins with this throw may slap his opponent's hands. If you win with 'Rock' this becomes a punch; while scissors are turned into a poke. This changes the dynamics of the game somewhat, in that players will favour one type of assault over another and hence try and win with that throw, so a player wary of being slapped again may try to overplay their opponent with scissors.

There are many variants of Extreme Rock, Paper, Scissors (ERPS) and each is referred to by different names in different countries. One of the most interesting is **Dancing RPS**, which can be played whilst dancing to music. Here, the three throws are Drum and Bass, Techno and, finally, Waltz. Techno (thrown by waving your arms in the air) beats Drum and Bass (hands make drumming motions), which in turn beats Waltz (arms are formed as if holding an imaginary partner for a waltz). To make the game fair, Waltz then beats Techno.

The French call RPS *Rochambeaux*. Presumably this inspired the television pro-gramme *South Park* to feature the game **Roshambo**, which involves male players taking it in turns to kick each other in the groin until one player falls down or gives up.

The well-known game of Rock, Paper, Scissors is hardly strange – although, strangely, it does have a World Championship (Bob 'the Rock' Cooper from the UK was the 2006 champion). However, if you consider yourself better than RPS, as its aficionados call it, you need to learn to play **Rock, Paper, Scissors 101** – the degree-level version.

This version of the game is played exactly like the game you know, except there are a phenomenal 101 possible hand positions. To make the game as random and fair as the standard game, each of the selected shapes beats fifty others, and can, in turn, be beaten by fifty itself. (Simple mathematics reveals that this will cause there to be a less than one percent chance of a tie and a total of 5 050 outcomes.)

The hand positions represent objects ranging from 'Alien' to 'UFO', 'Medusa' to

'Satan'. These are fully illustrated on the RPS 101 website (see Internet Resources) and range from the obvious hand movements to ones requiring some skill. (The shape for 'Vampire' is particularly brilliant.)

As an example of how the game plays, if you choose to go with 'Gun' this will shoot 'Princess', blast apart 'Turnip', but will be resisted by 'Dragon'. If you choose 'Baby', this will spill 'Beer', ruin 'Guitar' and be unaware of 'Satan', but is obviously carried off by 'Robot'.

Once you have mastered the 101 hand positions and memorised which other positions they beat, then comes the even harder part – finding someone to play against.

Finger Jousting

Finger Jousting, or Finger Fencing as it is sometimes known, is a possibly ancient game that combines jousting and sword fighting yet requires neither horse nor blade.

In its simplest form, two players stand facing each other and clasp their right hands together as if about to arm wrestle. Then, on a given command, each player extends his index finger (their 'lance') and battle commences. The objective is to jab your opponent before they jab you. At no point may the players' hands lose contact with each other. This means that jabbing the other player is often a lot less straightforward than you might initially think; with feints, sideways moves and full body twists all yielding results.

For a basic game, the first to score wins, or you can apportion different points for striking different body areas: legs and other arm gets one point, chest and back gets two points, the head gets three points. The jousting arm itself must never be hit, and the unused arm may play no part in the bout.

The game's governing body, the World Finger Jousting Federation (which is run by the self-styled Lord of the Joust, Julian Gluck) has built up a glossary of finger fighting terms and rules (see Internet Resources for website) which includes such gems as:

Bobbo Lance: A straight jousting move wherein a player cocks their right elbow back towards their chest, pulling their opponent closer.

Gesture of Good Disposition: A physical motion executed before and after every match as a sign of gratitude towards the opponent. Approved tournament gestures are handshakes, bows, head nods and man hugs.

Taking care of your fingernails is a sign of respect for your opponent and shows an interest in maintaining a healthy body.

The length of a competitor's finger shall not be longer than 15cm.

Illegal fingernail length is an automatic disqualification unless an approved glove is worn or the fingernail is trimmed immediately.

American-Indian Leg Wrestling

American-Indian Wrestling is based on pitting different parts of the body against your opponent's, one part at a time. There are many different forms, such as Back Wrestling: standing back to back and trying to push each other a set distance; One-legged Wrestling: standing on one leg and trying to push your opponent over; Thumb Wrestling, and, of course, **Leg Wrestling**.

In Leg Wrestling two players lie flat on their backs, side by side. They should be next to each other and touching, but pointing in different directions so that the feet of one player are next to the head of the other and the players' hips are touching. They then simultaneously raise their adjacent legs straight up three times. On the third raise players should hook ankles and try to pull their opponent over. No other part of the body is used, and the non-playing leg should remain flat on the floor and not be used for leverage. Games usually last a much shorter time than in Arm Wrestling, and successful play depends not just on muscular strength but also on stealth and speed.

Mora

Mora is an ancient guessing game that involves using your hands.

If there are two players, each faces the other and on a count of three must show a number of fingers on one hand. The number chosen can be anything from zero (keep your fist closed) to five (extend your thumb and all of your fingers). At the same time as both players show their hand they also shout out what they think the total number of fingers will be. If a player guesses correctly they gain two points; whoever is nearest to the correct answer gets one point.

A successful strategy involves noticing whether your opponent has a tendency to favour small or large numbers, then using this information appropriately.

Peanuts

A silly playground game, the finger-wrestling game of **Peanuts** at least has the advantage of developing your finger and wrist muscles.

Two players face each other, raise both their hands and interlink their fingers. With their hands clasped in this fashion, battle now commences as each attempts to bend back the other's hands and, obviously, avoid having their own bent. To make the game fair, hands need to be kept at shoulder height throughout. The game finishes when one player's hands are successfully bent back or one gives up with an anguished shout of 'peanuts'.

Pen Spinning

If you ever sit in your office or schoolroom bored out of your mind and twirling your pen around your fingers, perhaps now is the time to take this practice more seriously. Learn a new trick or two, because the serious finger-bending sport of **Pen Spinning** is a growing one.

Having originated in Japan, competitive pen spinning then spread to Korea and the US, and has now developed set moves such as rapid end to end passes, twirls, the thumbaround (the pen travels 360 degrees around the thumb), and nail spins (the pen spins on a fingernail), and even jumps. Keen pen spinners use specially modified and weighted pens, and to see a quality spinner in action is to see the hand working at the upper limits of its capabilities – fingers and pen both blur. The US-based Universal Pen Spinning Board (see Internet Resources) hold regular, videoed competitions where spinners are judged by their peers on style, tricks and overall routine.

Unfortunately, there is yet to be a serious take up of table-top finger drumming.

Shin Kicking

The Japanese have Judo; the Chinese have Kung Fu; in Gloucestershire they kick shins.

The **British Shin Kicking Championships** take place annually in Chipping Campden on the first Friday after the second May Bank Holiday as part of the Cotswold Olimpick Games. Dress rules are very simple and elegant: competitors wear long trousers with straw protective padding attached to their shins underneath (otherwise it would be plain crazy). White shepherds' smocks complete the fighting costume. Each player then holds onto his opponent's shoulders and the kicking begins.

Rules dictate that no kicks are allowed above knee level, and, whilst kicking, each player must try to wrestle his opponent to the ground. This has to be achieved during the process of kicking, otherwise it is not a valid wrestle down.

The long-since forgotten, but analogous, sport of Clog Shin Kicking was popular in the mining towns around Manchester in the mid-nineteenth century. Then, men were men and kicked shins whilst they were totally naked except for the heavy wooden clogs on their feet. Contests were hard fought and bloody. Some competitors bent the rules by soaping themselves up first, thus making themselves more difficult to grab hold of.

If Shin Kicking appeals but is a little too violent for your liking, you could always try the gentler, modern-day equivalent of **Toe Fencing**. In this sport players, once again, clasp each other by the shoulders but attempt to stamp on the other's toes before their own are squashed.

Slapsies

If Rock, Paper, Scissors is the king of playground hand games, **Slapsies**, or Slaps, is its boorish, dysfunctional half-brother who's heading for Borstal. There are records of it being played in the 1940s, but its popularity fluctuates and presently it is making something of a comeback.

For two people playing, both hold their hands as if praying but with arms stretched out in front of them and fingertips touching. Each then takes it in turn to try to slap the back of one of their opponent's hands before they can be withdrawn. If they succeed, they get another go. If they miss, their opponent has their turn, and so on.

If a player withdraws their hands three times when a slap has not been attempted, their opponent has a free slap (usually it is delivered with the utmost venom and is therefore very painful).

The term 'tipsies' is shouted if the striking player catches the fingertips of the slappee. This still counts as a hit and he gets another go.

Play continues until a player's will to go on disappears as his hands glow an ever deeper red.

Slapsies is in the unusual position of being a hand game with no official governing body and no organised championships as yet.

An interesting Slapsies variation is **My Mother Says**.

For two players: each places their hands alternately on top of one another's on a firm surface, such as a table, as if they were playing My Mother Says That You Are This High (where players all place their hands together in a pile then pull them out and on top whilst chanting the phrase, until the moment when one player's hand movement corresponds with 'High' and so becomes 'It'). Now, with their hands in position, the player whose hand is at the bottom must withdraw it as swiftly as possible and attempt a hard slap on the topmost hand. Obviously the player whose hand is exposed must try to withdraw it, avoiding the slap and hopefully causing the player in motion to slap his own hand with force. Play now alternates with the hand at the bottom of the pile having the next go. The faster the game is played, the more confusing, and often painful, it becomes.

There is a superb online computer simulation of Slapsies called **Operation Slaps**, which allows you to play slapsies virtually against a friend or against a computer opponent. In this online game you can decide to be one of five different characters, ranging from Lieutenant Lindequest (a cold and cruel female, Russian, Ground Force operative) to Sergeant Shaw (a well-hard marine from Guantánamo Bay). The action is accompanied by realistic slapping sounds, brooding atmospheric music and, of course, a pain meter.

Slapheads

The dull-witted game of **Slapheads** is like the human equivalent of the summer-fair game of Bash the Rat (when a 'rat' is dropped through a drainpipe and the player has to hit it with a baseball bat as it emerges).

In Slapheads, one person stands and hold their hands – palms facing inwards – shoulder-width apart. From a standing start the second player must now quickly move their head down between their opponent's hands and avoid being slapped. Whether it's through fear of reprisals or slowness of reactions, the slaphead often wins and the slappee is left slapping thin air.

During play the players should wear some sort of safety helmet. Encouraging people to play old-fashioned games to help in the fight against obesity is all well and good, but it should not be at the expense of a perforated eardrum.

Thumb Wrestling

Man's opposable thumbs were a giant evolutionary leap that enabled him to use a great many tools and separated him out from the lower animals. For example, in the twentieth century it was impossible to be a successful hitchhiker without one, and in more recent times mobile phone texting is infinitely harder if you don't use your thumb. But it is in the arena of wrestling where the thumb really comes into its own.

Thumb Wrestling, or Thumb Wars, is the easiest and least violent of all the hand games listed in this book. To play, you simply clasp your opponent's fingers and raise your thumb. Most games start with the now legendary chant: '1, 2, 3, 4, I declare a thumb war.' The game can now begin or, if you want to increase the tension further, you can chant: '5, 6, 7, 8, try to keep your thumb straight.'

Each player then tries to force their opponent's thumb down, and keep it down for a count of three. This is often a lot harder than it first appears, and a well-balanced match can last a long time and be quite tiring, especially if you have not trained your thumb up beforehand.

As you become more involved in the world of Thumb Wrestling, as well as training up your thumb muscles you may want to start dressing up your thumb – maybe as a well-known, real-life wrestler? A few strands of yellow wool glued to the back of your thumb nail and you have a Hulk Hogan. Or use some felt-tip pens to draw a Union Jack leotard on your knuckle and you'll have a pretty convincing Big Daddy.

Toe Wrestling

Toe Wrestling, a uniquely British take on arm wrestling, was invented in the 1970s in Ye Olde Royal Oak Inn, Staffordshire, and this is where the World Championships of this sport take place every year. Rumour and legend have it that it was invented primarily as a game at which Britain could be successful on the world stage. However, application for Olympic status was denied as the Olympic Committee couldn't decide whether it was a winter or summer game.

Whether or not any of the above is true, what can't be denied is that **Toe**

Wrestling is an exhilarating, strenuous sport and probably the most interesting way to catch athlete's foot in a competitive environment.

To play, competitors sit on the floor with their barefooted right leg extended towards their opponent. Heels are placed together and big toes locked ready for battle. As in its less exotic brother, Arm Wrestling, each player tries to force his opponent's foot down onto the ground using the most expedient method possible.

Each match consists of three ends; the first player to win two of these wins the contest.

If you want to avoid the chance of catching some pedopathic disease, you can always play the more pedestrian version of the game, **Slipper Wrestling**. Here, the same basic position is used except each competitor wears their slippers and the aim is to remove your opponent's footwear before they remove yours by the means of foot pressure, wriggling, and manipulation only. The smoking of a pipe whilst playing is optional.

Up Jenkins

Up Jenkins is an odd parlour game that deserves to be more widely known. What could be better than a game involving psychology, deception and violence, and all played around the dining-room table?

For two teams of three or more players each, one team sits down on one side of the table and is given a coin; the opposing team sits facing them on the other side. Team one now place their hands underneath the table and pass the coin between themselves until the leader of the opposing team shouts out, 'Up Jenkins'. Each player must simultaneously bring both their hands up with fists closed, and on the command of 'Down Jenkins' they must slam their hands, palms down, onto the table.

It is now the job of team two to start asking for hands to be turned over, with the aim of leaving the hand hiding the coin until last. If they are successful it is their turn with the coin next, if they fail they have to be the guessing team again. For variation, the guessing team can add the commands 'Crawl', where hiding players must crawl their hands forwards on the top of the table whilst trying to keep the coin hidden; and 'Fist', where they must form their hands into a fist. However, each of these can be requested only once in the game.

To play an extreme version, let the team member hiding the coin have a free slap of the opposing leader's hands if they guess incorrectly.

INDOOR GAMES

Now is the time to throw away your consoles and play odd games instead – in the privacy of your own home, of course. The games described here vary from ones that need just your own body and home environment to golf with citrus fruit and to the almost forgotten, but hopefully soon to be rediscovered, dangerous parlour game of Snapdragons.

Big Brother

If someone says to you, 'Let's play Big Brother', you will probably imagine a game that involves sitting around on sofas in a minimalist house, arguing over shopping lists and bitching about other players not being true to themselves. Or, if you are older, you may imagine a game involving a perspex helmet, a very hungry rat and lots of screaming.

Fortunately, this **Big Brother** is neither of these, just a great indoors game for two players. Each is given a rolled-up newspaper and then blindfolded. Players then

spin themselves around a set number of times to disorientate themselves but not make themselves too dizzy. Then they get down on their hands and knees.

Player one then shouts out, 'Are you there Big Brother?'. To this, player two must make the reply 'Yes'. Now player one can lash out with their rolled-up newspaper, their aim to make contact with the opponent. If they do, they immediately get another go until they miss. If they miss, it is the other player's turn. Once a player has responded, 'Yes', they are allowed to move or scuttle away as best they can, but they must remain on hands and knees at all times (and in this way hopefully avoid any incoming blows).

A great game, but probably not one to play against a skilled ventriloquist with a strong right arm...

Big Brother has similarities to the game **Are you there, Moriarty?** Here, two players are blindfolded and lie flat on their backs with the tops of their heads almost touching. Each is given a rolled-up newspaper or plastic sword. Player one calls out 'Are you there, Moriarty?', to which the opponent replies 'I'm here', and then either rolls to their right, left, or stays where they are. On hearing the reply player one immediately strikes out with their weapon and has to make the choice to hit directly above their head or to the right or left. If they succeed in hitting their opponent, player two goes back to their original place and player one retains the strike. If player one misses, it is player two's turn.

Another good variation on this game is **Blindfold Water Pistol Fighting**. Simply place two loaded water pistols in the centre of the room, then stand two players at the side of the room, blindfold them and set them off. Their first task will be to find their weapon, then they have to try to fire it in the direction of their opponent. The first player to shoot the other, wins. Non-playing partygoers add to the fun and confusion by shouting out directions to the players.

Kids' Games for Adults

Is there a better sight than that of a group of adults reliving their early childhood with a Bottom Shuffling Competition? There is much to be said for regressing to one's childhood whilst playing one of the inane, stupid games below.

Drinking Competition is an old party game. For two or more players at a time, each is given a cup of water and a teaspoon and the aim is to drink the water as quickly as possible using only the teaspoon. For adults, replace the water with an alcoholic drink or try a paired drinking competition: pair players up and give them each a drink and teaspoon, as before, but now they must feed each other simultaneously in the fastest time possible.

Human Knotting is a game that exemplifies the maxim 'the more the merrier' as everyone is tied up in knots. All players, bar one, link hands in a long line. Both ends of the line then begin to thread themselves through the others, pulling those behind them (always keeping hold of each others' hands) and continue in this way until a human knot has been created. The solitary player now has to unknot the rest of the players in the quickest time possible.

Collapsing Bridges is tremendous fun – as long as you don't have back problems or a phobia of being trapped under heavy weights.

For two evenly sized players; one makes the 'bridge' by kneeling on the floor and then placing their hands on the ground, leaving adequate space for the second player to crawl beneath their stomach. This second player crawls through a maximum of three times and the player being the bridge has to decide on one of those times to collapse (much of the excitement of the game is not knowing when this will happen). This they do by letting their weight take over and flopping onto the player crawling beneath them. The aim of the crawler is to get free in the quickest time possible. The bridge player cannot use arms and legs to keep the other trapped, but must use purely their weight.

Bucking Bronco has been played by every child at one time or another but few carry on playing to adulthood – which is a shame because it improves and gets much funnier as you get older. For two players, one plays the Bronco by kneeling on the floor and supporting their upper body with their arms. The rider now sits on them, not in the centre of the back but nearer the bottom, takes their feet off the floor and holds onto the collar of the Bronco with one hand only. It is now the Bronco's role to dislodge the rider in the quickest time using sudden movements, spins and turns, but keeping knees and hands on the floor at all times.

Banana Racing

Banana Racing is simplicity itself and great to play on a polished floor.

Slide one foot as far forward as you are able, as if slipping on a discarded banana skin. Then drag the trailing foot back up to meet the first. Both of your feet must remain touching the ground at all times. Once you have mastered the required feet movements, you need to practise increasing the speed – obviously the faster the better. And remember, if you are playing this outside the official shoes of the Banana Racer are not training shoes or sneakers but a pair of leather-soled brogues.

To play real banana racing you will need… bananas. Eat the insides then use strong rubber bands to attach the skins, slippy-side exposed, to the base of your shoes. Competitors now race to complete a course in the quickest time whilst avoiding falling. Possibly the only game around in which you can boost your potassium levels and risk a serious hamstring injury all at the same time.

Blood Potato

Combine Blindman's Buff with Murder in the Dark and you get not 'Buff Blindman in the Dark', but **Blood Potato** – a superb indoor game. This is rarely seen played at parties, but it is reasonably common at drama schools (presumably it is popular with all the budding Bela Lugosis).

All players are blindfolded and one of them is given the role of murderer (without anyone else knowing who that person is). Players then start to move around the room. If two meet they must say the word 'potato' to each other; however, if the murderer meets someone, instead of saying 'potato' he must say the word 'blood', upon which they must scream dramatically, die, and remove themselves from the game by standing at the edge of the room. The game continues, with the body count increasing and fear levels rising until no 'potatoes' are left.

The game is improved immeasurably if eliminated players encourage and shout warnings and directions to the remaining players.

Living Room Challenges

Often the best indoor games are those that require little or no equipment except your own body and a wish to test it to its limits.

Furthest Coin is a fun game for players of similar height. The object of the game is to place a coin on the floor as far away from your feet as possible and then pick it up again.

However, you cannot move your feet from their starting position, and, to reach as far as possible, you can support your body only with your non-coin-holding hand. Once the coin has been placed, the players must now return to a standing position in a similar one-armed fashion. To complete the game, all players now have to recover their coins using the same method. The winner is the player who manages to place, and successfully retrieve, a coin the furthest distance from their feet.

Another great indoor game for players of similar height is **Furthest From the Wall**. Taking turns, each player must stand some distance from a wall and then lean forward towards it and support themselves (to avoid crashing head first into the wall) with ONE arm only. Their feet must remain together and in a fixed position. To complete their turn they must get back to the upright position by pushing hard off the wall, again using one hand only. No step-backs are allowed and the feet must remain in a fixed position throughout.

Players continue to take turns, each time trying to get further back from the wall. The one who successfully completes the manoeuvre with his feet the biggest distance away is the winner.

Drawing Room Baseball

An extremely silly indoor game, but immense fun nonetheless, **Drawing Room Baseball** brings the great American sport into the living room and provides hours of endless amusement and broken ornaments.

This game is best played with small teams of three or four players (but it does depend on how big your house is). Simply re-arrange some room furnishings (cushions, chairs, etc.) to provide the bases, then replace the baseball bat with a kitchen spatula (either wood or metal) and instead of a baseball use a Ping-Pong ball. This gives the pitcher the opportunity to wind up their throwing arm and pitch the ball as hard as they want without fear of injury. Any damage to the room is not from bat and ball action, but rather the dashes to reach bases and the scrambles for the ball of the fielding team.

Bucket Ball

Bucket Ball has a similar feel to Hanetball (see page 180), in the sense that the player actually stands within the goal but it is much weirder, more fun and... uses buckets.

For two competing players, at the start of the game each player stands facing the other, a few yards apart. Both have placed their feet into plastic buckets, one on each foot. If children are playing a standard bucket is usually perfect; for adult players you may need to search a garden centre for larger specimens.

Players hold in their hands an equal number of small balls. The aim of the game is to throw as many balls as possible into either of your opponents' buckets, whilst avoiding getting too many in your own. Players are allowed to move about, so the game soon develops into tense stand-offs, daring bucket-footed attacks, and desperately clumsy leg movements to avoid incoming balls landing in one of your own buckets. Any player falling over loses, and once all the balls have been thrown the bucket-balls should be added up to determine the winner.

Elbow Racing

Unless you have access to knee and elbow protectors, the old Inuit game of **Elbow Racing** (*Ikusimmiaq*) is probably best played inside on a thick carpet.

To play, simply crouch down on your knees, place both elbows on the floor and both hands over your ears. Now, maintaining this position – race. You can not remove your hands from your ears and you must propel yourself forwards using only your knees and elbows.

The fastest person over the course, or, more usually, the person who can stop laughing the longest, wins.

Faceball

Every so often the human brain surpasses itself with its ingenuity and invents a game so sublime that Olympic status can surely only be months away. **Faceball** is one such game.

Created by the staff at *Flickr.com*, the game of Faceball is like a stationary version of dodgeball, but much more fun.

For two players; each sits on an office chair ten feet from the other. Players then take it in turns to throw a beach-ball-type ball at their opponent's face. If they manage a successful strike they gain a point, retrieve the ball and throw again. If they miss, it's their opponent's turn. Target players may not move to avoid the ball but must remain still whilst the other throws. Points accumulate with each strike over a set number of rounds.

An alternative version of Faceball exists which is more of a cross between Faceball and Wallhooky (see page 44). Simply get a soft ball and attach some string to it, a little like the string and ball part of a Swingball set, and fix it to the ceiling. The height should be adjusted so that when the string is at about 60 degrees to the vertical the ball will be at the competitors face height. Two players now stand either side of the dangling ball and set it swinging in a circular motion. They then take it in turns to flap at the ball with their hand, when it is closest to them, so that if they make contact it swings and strikes their opponent in the face. Simple. The most scores, out of ten attempts, wins.

House Gymnastics

Many children attempt the task of climbing up the inside of a door frame by placing one foot on either side at the base and gradually shuffling up until they reach the top. **House Gymnastics** starts with this basic idea and goes further. Much further.

House Gymnastics was created and developed by two men taking the names Harrison and Ford. The legend has it that they came up with the idea after a thwarted attempt to put up a window blind. An hour or two of sweating and swearing in a

cramped space, drilling holes whilst deciphering instructions, and a legendary strange game is born. In its purest form House Gymnastics is that perfect combination of yoga, gymnastics and art.

Harrison and Ford have developed a wonderful array of positions that can be achieved throughout the house using only the human body and the house fittings and fixtures. The previously mentioned 'door wedge' is present and correct, as is 'the banister snake', which involves bracing yourself horizontally along an upstairs banister rail, and 'the ceiling stand', a handstand on the banister with the feet braced against the ceiling. All manner of squeezing, bracing and balancing of the human form within a house can be seen on their website (see Internet Resources) and they have been given great names such as the Elevated Carpet Crab, the One-handed Starfish and the Backdoor Bat Hang, with each position given a difficulty rating.

The ultimate indoor gymnastics position is known as the XXX (after the Vin Diesel film). To do it you need two adjacent walls that are the same distance apart as your own height when your arms are held above your head. A corridor is often an ideal location. Next, you need to climb slowly with your feet on one wall and your hands against the other, so that you end up perfectly horizontal, outstretched, spanning the corridor but with your back as near the ceiling as possible.

The positions should be held for at least three seconds, but obviously you gain more kudos if you can remain wedged on the top shelf of a bookcase for longer. Moves and positions can also be taken out of the confines of the house and have been performed in the office, sports stadia and the great outdoors.

Indoor Games with Biscuits

Malteser Blow Football is the perfect game for football-fixated chocoholics.

Make two teams of two players each. One player from each team makes the goal by kneeling down on opposite sides of a small table so that their bottom lips are at table level; they now open their mouths as wide as possible. Their teammates stand on the other side and compete, using straws to blow a Malteser into their goal while defending the other.

Biscuit Dunking is a subject that causes much debate amongst biscuit connoisseurs; such as whether a biscuit should be dunked in a cup of tea and, if it should, which varieties are able to withstand the process best without disintegrating.

There is no authoritative biscuit-dunking body; to hold your own competition you just need each player to pick their biscuit of choice and stand by a steaming hot cup of tea. All players now simultaneously repeatedly dunk, making sure at least half of the biscuit is submerged each time. The last biscuit to show any damage wins. The radio station XFM held a World Championship Biscuit Dunking Competition in September 2007 over a three-week period. The biscuits making the final were the Caramel Wafer, Fig Roll, Digestive Caramel and the winner, the hardy Pink Wafer.

Biscuit Bobbing is a party game that is less healthy than its apple-based cousin but just as much fun and, if anything, more difficult. Place some biscuits (digestives work well) flat down on a table and then players must try to eat a whole biscuit in the fastest time without using their hands in any way. The difficulty lies in getting hold of the biscuit in the first place – a feat usually achieved by lifting it with the teeth. The game is improved immeasurably if everyone plays at once, leading to a chaotic biscuit scrum. More advanced players could try playing the game with something thinner, such as an oatcake.

Crazy Stair Climbing

Crazy Stair Climbing is the perfect name for what appears to be a more mobile branch of House Gymnastics. All that is required is a narrow stairwell with strong banister rails on each side and some imagination. A variety of methods can be used to traverse either up or down the stairs, but at no time must your feet touch the ground.

The basic Crab method involves holding onto the banister rail with both hands, placing your feet against the wall below, then 'walking' in a hand-over-hand style down the stairs, keeping toes off the ground at all times. With one player on each rail, this makes for a grand race.

For single players, the Crab Straddle involves placing a foot on top of each rail and then, by stretching forwards, placing your hands on the rails too. In this straddle position you now have to shuffle upwards to get to the top of the stairs as quickly as possible. Once mastered, the next step (sic) is the Downhill Crab Straddle. Something only for the bravest stair climbers, this is exactly the same but involves moving head first down the stairs.

Airplanes

Airplanes (1) is a trick game that can probably only be played once, unless you keep participants out of the room until it is their turn. Two strong players are required to hold a plank of wood at hip height a few feet above the floor. The partygoer who is playing the pilot is shown the plank then blindfolded and helped onto it. They stand there and support themselves by placing their hands on the shoulders of the two carriers, who then proceed to walk the plank around the room. These carriers then carefully kneel down so that the plank is as close to the floor as possible. To the partygoer, whose hands remain on their shoulders, it appears if anything that they are lifting him higher above the floor. The carriers then announce that the plane is about to crash and the pilot needs to parachute to safety. What feels to the blindfolded pilot to be a metre or so is merely a matter of centimetres. Will they dare to jump?

Airplanes (2) is an Inuit game of strength. In teams of four players, one forms the airplane by lying face down on the floor with their feet together and arms outstretched. The other three teammates now pick up this player, one holding his ankles, the others holding a forearm each. The airplane player must now keep their body totally rigid for as long as possible whilst teammates 'fly' them across the room. The team that achieves the greatest distance, before the airplane gives up and begs their teammates to stop, wins.

Firing Squad

You can't beat the addition of a lighted candle to a game to bring that extra element of danger.

Firing Squad is for two or more players at a time. Players fix a candle to the top of a cycle helmet using molten wax, then strap the helmets to their heads. The candles are now lit. Each player is given a fully loaded water pistol and their aim is to extinguish the other's flame in the quickest time possible. The last person to retain a lit candle is the winner. Players can move about to avoid incoming water, although they must do so cautiously as this increases the risk of the candle going out through their own movements.

For even greater fun, play at night with the lights out.

Grasshopper

Fun indoor games based on hit television shows are few and far between – Blind Man's Buffy the Vampire Slayer was never going to be a big hit at children's parties. But **Grasshopper**, a game based around one crucial scene in the hit 70s show *Kung Fu*, is the TV-to-indoor-game conversion that really works.

Simply get a long roll of bubble wrap and lay a path out on top of a solid floor. Players now take it in turns to walk barefooted along the length of bubblewrap – just like Kwai Chang Caine (Grasshopper) did on rice paper in *Kung Fu*. In the series, under the direction of his mentor Master Po, he would try almost painfully hard to walk delicately down the paper only to get to the end, turn around, and see rips galore. He only achieved a perfect walk once he had reached true lightness of spirit through his Kung Fu training.

So any player who is heard to pop a bubble is out until it's his turn again – or you can simply count the pops each player makes and add a time penalty for each one. Players must aim to walk along the bubble path as stylishly as possible with as much Zen poise and balance as Kwai Chang himself.

To add to the game, place a candle at the end of the path for the Kung Fu master to place his hand in the flame and yet feel no pain.

Atmosphere is added if a non-player can commentate on proceedings using the wise words of Master Po: '*It is only through a lightness of mind and spirit, Grasshopper, that your feet will leave no mark.*'

Heinz and Seek

Dragging uncooperative children around the supermarket is hell at the best of times. **Heinz and Seek** is the perfect game that is guaranteed to keep squalling siblings entertained all the way from the cheese counter to the checkout.

Very simply, one parent enters the supermarket first and moves an item (one that is easily recognisable by all players – such as a branded tin of baked beans, packet of crisps, etc.). The item must now be placed somewhere else in the store, in an incongruous place but at a reasonable height for all the players to find.

The rest of the family then go into the store and are told what the product is that they are looking for. Whilst shopping, the seeking players must find the moved item before reaching the checkout.

Obviously this is not a game that you would want all the shoppers in the supermarket to play simultaneously, otherwise it would turn food shopping into a totally random experience.

Strange Jumping Games

Inuit culture has produced many fantastic games, but with **Tiliraginik Qiriqtagtut**, or the slightly easier to say **Jump Over Stick**, they have created one of the great strange games that requires athleticism, jumping ability and the ownership of a good stick.

To play, get a solid stick (a broom handle works well) and hold it in both hands in front of your body. Hands should be shoulder-width apart. The objective is to jump both feet off the ground at once and over the stick, without releasing your grip, and land without toppling. You should now be in a slightly crouched position

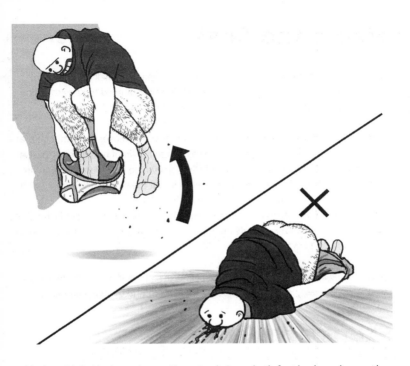

with the stick behind your knees. Now simply jump both feet backwards over the stick to return to your starting position. Repeat until exhausted.

There is a modern-day equivalent of Jump Over Stick, namely **Underpants Jumping** (or the Sport of Philanderers, as it is sometimes known). Keep your clothes on and use a spare pair of underpants (old ones where the elastic has gone may be the best, but whichever you choose, avoid the use of the thong). To play the game, hold the pants in front of your body and jump both feet simultaneously into them, then pull them up to your waist, take them off and jump again. Players play against the clock to see who can do the most underpants jumps within a set time.

Minesweepers

Minesweepers is the modern name for a game which used to be known as Battle of the Atlantic. There is nothing to beat the thrill of imagining yourself as the Admiral of a fleet crossing the Atlantic, dodging mines and Nazi U-boats.

A largish, clear space is needed for the best game. In this space, scatter as many tennis balls as possible – the game works well if the floor has a good covering of them. Players are then paired up and one member of the team is blindfolded. The seeing player must then navigate their partner ('ship') from one side of the room to the other, through the barrage of tennis balls ('mines') but can only direct them by shouting. If a ship touches a mine the watching players shout 'BANG', and the team have a time penalty added. If the ship touches five mines, it is sunk. Players that get from one end of the room to the other in the fastest time, win.

To make the game more authentic, you can allow only nautical directions such as, 'full steam ahead', 'avast', 'port', and 'starboard' to be given to the blindfolded player.

Scuds and Patriots

You have a floor covered with lots of tennis balls, teams paired up and ready to go, yet the game Minesweepers, although tasteless, has paradoxically lost some of its flavour. What you need to play is **Scuds and Patriots**.

If you're setting up from scratch, as in Minesweepers, you need to scatter as many tennis balls as possible over the floor – a large room or hall makes an ideal venue. Now team players up into twos and blindfold one player from each pair. In Scuds and Patriots two teams play at once. One blindfolded player, the 'Scud', starts from one side of the room and, as before, must try to get to the opposite side without stepping on tennis balls. They are aided in this navigation by the shouted directions of their teammate. The other team's blindfolded player, the 'Patriot', is positioned on a side wall, halfway down the room. Once the 'Scud' has traversed a third or so of the way, the 'Patriot' is released. Their aim, again guided by their own partner and again avoiding stepping on balls, is to make contact with the 'Scud' and in doing so win the game. If the 'Scud' reaches the far wall that team wins.

If either player steps on a ball then they have to remain still for the count of five or, for more confusion, spin around on the spot five times. Non-playing spectators are free to provide any sound effects they think appropriate.

Lemon Golf

Lemon Golf is the best use for a lemon outside of perking up a gin and tonic or removing scum stains from the inside rim of a toilet – and it's a wonderful party game.

To play, give all competitors a lemon (their 'golf' ball) and a golf putter. The aim of the game, as in real golf, is to knock your lemon around the course in the fewest strokes, which, here, is made more fun by the random nature of the lemon's movement. The course is created by positioning upturned paper cups (the holes) around the room. And don't forget hazards: a sheepskin rug makes a marvellous rough, a scattering of sand could form a bunker.

In these days of health and safety madness it may be advisable for players to wear safety glasses, as one overhit lemon could easily result in a nasty lemon juice in the eye incident.

Sniper

Sniper is a bizarre marriage of apple bobbing and hula-hoop dancing. An apple is tied to a length of string (60–90cm works well) and this is then attached to a belt so that when worn the apple will dangle down at the front of the wearer.

Another player then holds up a plank at waist height through which a long nail has been hammered. Players then take it in turns to wear the belt and by spinning around they try to impale the apple upon the nail. The player who impales their apple in the quickest time is the winner.

There are two schools of thought on the most effective technique for this game: there are the players who try to line up the nail with the apple then fire the fruit with a Shakira-like flick of the hips, and then there are the 'whirling dervishes' who spin around frantically with the apple as a crazed satellite – frankly a danger to both themselves and anyone in the firing line.

Three Table-top Games

Imagine, if you will: there is a thunderstorm outside, all the power in the house is out and all the batteries in the children's Nintendos and iPods have mysteriously gone flat. How will you ever keep them entertained? The answer lies in the use of the dining-room table and three of the finest table-top games ever invented.

To play **Thimble Soccer,** clear the table and give each player four thimbles. These should be worn on the index and middle fingers of each hand and will form the boots on the footballers' feet. Raid the sewing box again for cotton reels to use as goalposts. A table-tennis ball is fine as the football. The obligatory rule is that players must keep all thimble-clad fingers on the table when the ball is in play; they must not lift their fingers or slide them around but must walk or run to get to the ball. (It's a fascinating way to discover whether you are two-footed and learn how to dribble.) And, of course, fouling and playacting can all play their part in the game.

Table Hockey recreates the sport of ice hockey but by using only a dining-room table and some cutlery. Use an old table that doesn't mind if it gets a scratch or two, a supply of tablespoons, some Blu Tack to form the goals and a checkers counter for the ball. Each player uses his tablespoon to dribble and pass the puck (quite difficult skills to acquire) with the ultimate aim being to propel it into the opponent's goal. As in real ice hockey, there are frequent clashes as players fight over the same puck and, again just as in the real game, if a fight develops you have a handy weapon readily available.

A massively popular game in America since the 1930s, **Paper Football** is virtually unheard of in the UK. It is best described as what you would get if you mixed origami with Subbuteo and added conversions and field goals. Any smooth table is suitable to form the pitch, whilst the football is formed from an A4 piece of paper, which with the correct folds can be formed into a small, flat, isosceles tri-angular ball.

Kick-offs are made by holding the 'ball' in the palm of your hand and throwing it into the opponent's half; where it lands is where they start. Players then take it in turns to flick the triangle, aiming for it to finish with any part of it hanging over the opposite edge of the table – a touchdown. This will win you six points. If no part of the triangle is over the edge it is the other player's turn. If a player scores a touchdown they can then attempt a conversion. Their opponent makes the goalposts by holding out both hands with their thumbs together and index fingers pointing upwards. The shooting player holds the ball in their palm and tries to flick it over the posts.

The Paper Football Association, the game's governing body (see Internet Resources), has a full set of instructions for play, including the very sensible advice to wear safety glasses when defending against a field goal!

Walking Trippy

A children's indoor or party game, **Walking Trippy** has been called a supreme game of skill and elegance, the English Gentleman's martial art and… bloody stupid.

The game is for two people. Each walks towards the other at a reasonable strolling pace and in a direction so that they would pass each other quite closely. The aim, however, is to trip up the other person as you pass. No use of the hand or arm is allowed and, most importantly, one mustn't break one's step; the trip must be accomplished by delicately catching the opponent's ankle or toes as he passes. Players must never stop walking when they meet, and if both players fail to trip the other they must carry on until they reach their opponent's starting point and then turn around, ready to play again.

It's a terrific game requiring large amounts of ankle and foot dexterity alongside feline-like balance. You gain one point if you make your opponent stumble and two points if they fall.

Charlie Chaplin Walking Trippy is a silent-movie variant of the game. This version involves adopting the bow-legged swagger of the movie star and twirling a cane or rolled-up umbrella. This additional weapon can be carried upside down, allowing the use of the curved handle to catch an ankle as you pass.

Ringing the Bull/Wallhooky

Simple to set up and play, but quite addictive, **Ringing the Bull** (or **Wallhooky**, as it is sometimes known) is an ancient pub game which was reputedly introduced to England by the Crusaders. Along with spices, carpets and writing paper, they brought back a game that involves a brass ring and a stuffed animal head with a hook attached to its nose. The game retains its popularity in the North of

England and the Caribbean, which was presented with it by early settlers.
To play, attach a bull's nose ring to a string from the ceiling and then attach a
hook to the wall in such a position that the bull's ring will hook on with the
string remaining taut. (Traditionally the hook was fitted to the nose of a stuffed
animal's head mounted on the wall.) Each player stands in the pre-determined
throwing position and has a set number of throws to get the ring hooked. The
player with the highest number of rings hooked is the victor.

Extra points can be scored for throws that perform a complete circle before getting hooked, but you are talking advanced Wallhooky there.

Mangel-wurzel Skittles

Mangel-wurzel Skittles is an ancient British West Country pub game that has
those twin magic ingredients of simplicity and stupidity.

A mangel-wurzel (a large beetroot-like vegetable) has a rope tied to it which is
attached to the ceiling of the room. The skittles are created by players standing
on narrow 15cm-high wooden blocks. Players are best arranged in a traditional
diamond formation. Which person gets which podium can be decided by drawing
straws. The mangel-thrower then launches the mangel-wurzel into the skittles. Players
take it in turn, as in normal skittles, to knock over as many people as possible.

Walnut Fighting

The great disadvantage of conker fighting is its seasonal nature, so if you find
yourself longing for a game outside of autumn you should learn the joys of
conker fighting's long-lost cousin, **Walnut Fighting**.

Walnut Fighting – the true king of seed-related fight games – was last big around the 1900s, and not many people today realise the fun that can be had with just some empy walnut shells.

To play, you need to crack open some walnuts and eat the nuts inside so that you end up with at least two undamaged half shells. A player takes a shell and places it flat-part down on the table. Their opponent does the same so that the pointed parts of the shells are touching. By applying pressure on the back of the shells, each player then tries to force their opponent's to crack. The first shell to shatter, or just crack, loses.

In the late eighteenth century the shells of snails were used in a similar contest called **Conquering Shells**. Shells were pressed against each other as above and the first to crack lost. Obviously, if you wanted to revive this game today you would have to use empty snail shells. A pan of snails fried gently in garlic butter makes a perfect pre-game meal.

Snapdragons

On Christmas Eve many families try to decide which game to play. Either a classic board game, a cosy parlour game or maybe even a DVD quiz game. Please don't make those mistakes, there is only one game for Christmas Eve: **Snapdragons**.

Very popular from the sixteenth to the nineteenth centuries, Snapdragons, or Flapdragons as it is also known, has explicably declined in popularity.

All you need to play is a bowl, some matches, raisins and brandy... and the address of your nearest accident and emergency department. Gather everyone around the dining-room table, place a large flat dish in the centre and into this scatter a good handful of raisins. Pour a layer of brandy or cognac over the dried

fruit, then set fire to the brandy and dim the lights. Players take it in turns to pluck a raisin out of the burning liquid and quickly eat it.

For a more competitive edge to the game, use larger dried fruit such as apricots, and stuff one of these with a lucky sixpence.

Shoeing the Wild Mare

Shoeing the Wild Mare is a traditional and totally mad Christmas game that goes back to at least the early seventeenth century.

To play, get a strong wooden beam, a few centimetres wide, and suspend it from the roof by two ropes of even length. The beam is the 'mare' of the title and should be level, yet high enough above the floor so that the players' feet are off the ground. A player, 'the farrier', then sits on the 'mare' in the centre, a leg on either side. This player has a hammer and has to give the underside of the beam 'four time eight blows' at a designated spot. If they fall off, it is someone else's turn.

Much hilarity, and the odd broken shoulder ensues.

Shoeing the Mare appears in its own nursery rhyme, Shoeing:

Shoe the colt,
Shoe the colt,
Shoe the wild mare;
Here a nail,
There a nail,
Yet she goes bare.

Balance, Burn and Splash

Balance, Burn and Splash is a medieval game that is a combination of Snapdragons and Shoeing the Wild Mare. It is hardly an overstatement to say that this game is due a revival, as it probably hasn't been played in the last five hundred years.

To play, simply place a narrow plank on two trestles. In the centre, underneath the plank, position a large tub or pool full of water. At one end of the plank place a lighted candle. Players must now balance themselves in the middle of the plank, above the water, holding an unlit candle, and must try to light it by stretching and shuffling towards the lit one, then return to their starting position whilst keeping their candle burning. Any player who puts a foot down or falls into the tub is out and it is the next player's turn.

OUTDOOR GAMES

Ah, the great outdoors: fresh air, unspoilt countryside, amazing views, flicking sponges of beer into people's faces… Yes, the outdoors has it all, and included here are some of the most unusual games you can play in the open air.

Three Three-legged Games

Nothing beats that slightly helpless feeling you get when you have your leg tied tightly to a partner's. For an adult **Three-legged Butterfly Hunting** is one of the quickest ways to feel like a child again, and the easiest route to spraining an ankle and a drive to casualty.

In Three-legged Butterfly Hunting players are paired up, legs are tied and then each team is given one butterfly net between them. The aim is that, by working together as a team, you catch a member of the order *Lepidoptera* (a butterfly). The last team to catch one, loses.

This is a delightful summer-garden party game for adults to play, especially if they have had a couple of glasses of Pimm's beforehand. The sight of two people tumbling helplessly into a buddleia bush is one to be treasured.

Although frisbee golf is considered a serious sport in some parts of the world, **Three-legged Frisbee Golf** is superior in almost every way.

For teams of two players, tie together the legs of playing pairs and give them a frisbee. On a starting command, all teams set off by throwing their frisbee, chasing after it as quickly as possible, picking it up and then throwing it again. The first team to get their frisbee to the 'hole' (a pre-determined object as far away as you like), wins.

A useful variation is Zombie Three-legged Frisbee Golf. After the starting throw, a team can either carry on trying to finish quickly or aim their frisbee at a competing couple. If they score a hit, that couple falls over 'dead'. This adds a further competitive and chance element to an already great game.

Three-legged Monster Chase is a game that requires large groups of people. Pairs are formed and have their legs bound together as usual. Each pair is then given a sheet of coloured stickers – a different colour for each team. On a starting command, the players set off, their objective being to place their stickers on the backs of their competitors and avoid being 'stickered' themselves. After a set time of pandemonium, play stops and the team that have been stickered the least, wins.

One-legged Tug-of-War and Other Odd-legged Games

The ability to balance perfectly on one leg is a skill perfected in the animal kingdom by the flamingo, but fortunately it is one that humans have never really had to master – unless, of course, you want to excel at the games below.

One-legged Tug-of-War is played in the same way as the standard version of Tug-of-War. A rope and two equal teams of similar-sized players are all that are required. At the start of the game all players lift one leg off the ground and start to pull. The skill of hopping and pulling a rope at the same time is one that not many people naturally possess – as you will soon discover if you play.

Any person putting a foot down is eliminated from that team. Play continues until victory is achieved or there is only one man still standing.

Cock Fighting is a quite violent game for two or more players. Here, players must hop around with arms crossed in a loose simulation of a cockerel. The aim of the game is to knock into your opponents or otherwise put them off so that they place their other leg down. Any player that puts down a leg is instantly out. The game can have a tendency to get quite rough, but is often won by the person skilled in making quick one-legged changes of directions that cause an attacker to go flying past and crash to the floor.

The game of **Dodgems**, a more brutal version of Cock Fighting, is a little like competitive pogo dancing, but it is one that was played long before Sid Vicious gave his dance to the world.

For as large a group of players as possible, all players fold their arms but stand on two feet. However, both legs must stay pressed together throughout the game. Players can then use any means left open to them to knock other players over. If you are knocked over or you unfold your arms, you withdraw from the game.

For more one-legged fun, try the elemental, childish fun that is a **Dizzy Hopping Race**. All competitors spin around a set number of times, sufficient to make them dizzy, then balance on one leg and hop as quickly as possible to the finishing line. This is an especially good game to play in an enclosed space, an ideal location being a corridor.

Wheelbarrow Games

In **Human Wheelbarrow Racing** one player walks on their hands whilst a team-mate grabs hold of their ankles and pushes them along. It used to be a ubiquitous event at every school sports day, but now, due to health and safety harridans and concerns about offending any obscure wheelbarrow-worshipping religions, it is almost a thing of the past. All that is needed to rejuvenate the marvellous world of wheelbarrow racing is a makeover, and some new variations.

Blindfolded Wheelbarrow Racing is a chaotic version of the classic race, working well with as many competitors as possible. Pair up the players – one barrow and one pusher – then blindfold the pusher. Once the race is underway, it is the wheelbarrow's job to shout out directions to their handler, often in a panicked voice, so that they can avoid clashing with other racers and get to the finishing line first.

To play **Underwater Wheelbarrow Racing** you need to find water of the correct depth – either calm shallows at the beach or a toddlers' paddling pool. The player who is the wheelbarrow puts on a mask and snorkel and is held by the pusher so that their head is underneath the water but they can breathe through the snorkel. Then the race is on to find the 25m Underwater Wheelbarrow Racing Champion.

Fantastic **Wheelbarrow Jousting** events can be held with just a little preparation. Create lances from the cardboard tubes inside rolls of kitchen foil, or make your own with rolled-up newspapers, then attach them to the top of a cycle helmet using masking tape. Two players then wear the head-lance helmets and are quickly pushed past each other by the wheelbarrow holders, the aim being to strike the other player on the head as they pass.

Dwile Flunking

Resurrected in the late 1960s, **Dwile Flunking** is an outdoor pub game of dubious origin but startling originality. Centred around the villages of Bungay and Beccles, in Suffolk, this is a bizarre game made even more unusual by its incredible array of yokel terminology.

The game requires two teams formed of twelve players each. One team forms a circle (called the Girter). A member of the opposing team takes their turn to stand in the middle of the Girter and be the Flonker. The Flonker carries a long stick (or

Driveller), on the end of which is a beer-sodden sponge (or Dwile). As the Girter members dance around them the Flonker must flonk their Dwile using the Driveller to try to hit a member of the Girter. They have two attempts and score as follows:

Hit on the head (known as a Wanton): three points.
Hit on the body (a Marther): two points.
Hit on the leg (a Ripple): one point.

Miss totally (a Swadger): no points, plus the poor Flonker must now, as a forfeit, quickly drink a pint of ale. A process which, for some reason, has no rustic alternative name in the yokel lexicon.

Each member of the team has a go at being the Flonker, then the two teams change places. The highest combined team score wins, although often games finish with no-one knowing or even caring about the score.

Like many village games, Dwile Flunking's origins are cloudy to say the least, but a game very similar in appearance appears in the sixteenth-century painting *Children's Games* by Bruegel.

Extreme Ironing

If you are looking to participate in a strange, outdoors extreme sport, you want something that is dangerous and esoteric and which transports you to exotic locales, while all the time keeping pin-sharp creases in your trousers. **Extreme Ironing** is the only sport that fits all the above categories and is, as the official website (see Internet Resources) so eloquently states, 'The latest danger sport that combines the thrills of an extreme outdoor activity with the satisfaction of a well-pressed shirt'.

Extreme Ironing was devised by Phil Shaw (aka 'Steam') a clothing-factory worker from Leicester. Faced with a large pile of clothes to iron when he would rather have been out rock climbing, he decided to combine the two activities and Extreme Ironing was born. After a trial in his back garden with his accomplice, 'Spray', he has taken the sport around the world (for some strange reason it is particularly popular in Germany, even though everyone knows that lederhosen don't need pressing).

The basic, and genuinely genius, idea is to iron (using a hot iron, if possible) an item of clothing on an ironing board in an extreme location. Locations have included mountains, whilst ski-ing, whilst nude, and even underwater. There are even people who have tried to iron whilst bungee jumping. One of Steam's greatest ironing moments came when, in Leicester city centre, he recreated David Blaine's Perspex box stunt by being suspended 15m above the ground – but with an ironing board.

However, all is not crease-free in the world of Extreme Ironing. There is rivalry between the Extreme Ironing Bureau and the breakaway Urban Housework Group who, instead of the joy of steam and starch, prefer to Hoover in the great outdoors.

The inaugural Extreme Ironing World Championships took place in Germany in 2002 with German competitor 'Hot Pants' taking the individual prize. And as the event continues to grow there is even talk of trying to get it recognised as an Olympic sport.

Extreme Poker

Extreme Poker is a superb combination in which the familiar card game is linked with a series of extreme sports and conditions. The extremity of the conditions change the dynamic of the game, as players are unaware whether others' behaviour is because of the cards they are holding or the fact that they are petrified of heights.

Begun by the company *Interpoker.com* with a poker game played outside on an ice sheet in the Arctic, play was as normal, except every time you were eliminated from a game you could buy your way back in by taking off an item of clothing. In subsequent years there have been games played in a variety of extreme environments, including one played in a jet at 9144m in which players wore parachutes and losers were required to jump out of the plane.

In Sydney in 2007 the event was staged on a specially built platform attached to the side of a cliff, 90m above the rocks below. Losers had to abseil off the platform. This, however, was only a qualifying event; the final was held underwater with players in full scuba gear. It is hard to tell if someone is making a face because they are bluffing or they have just spotted a shark.

Fruit and Vegetable Croquet

It's not often that you find a game that is so awe-inspiringly brilliant that it makes you wonder why you ever played anything else; a game that combines food with sexual hip thrusts and then turns it into a competition. **Fruit and Vegetable Croquet** is one such game.

Each player obtains an old pair of ladies' tights and places a heavy vegetable or fruit down one of the legs. (Experiment with varieties such as butternut squashes or maybe a nice juicy melon.) The tights are then tied about the waist of the player so that the dangling fruit hangs near ground level between his legs. An orange is substituted for the croquet ball. The aim of the game is for each player to swing the laden tights between his legs so that the fruit inside strikes the orange and sends it in the direction required and, preferably, through a hoop. All the normal rules of croquet apply.

The sight of someone swinging their hips as if they are in some sort of bizarre hip-hop video in order to get a nylon-enclosed dangling squash to hit an orange is a sight that, if seen only once, will stay burned in your brain for a very long time.

Human Croquet, Human Boules and Human Curling

It's a lazy August afternoon and you are sitting on the veranda sipping a cool Pimm's when the party host shouts, 'Anyone for Human Croquet?'

To play **Human Croquet,** the perfect summer garden game, you need to pair up all of the partygoers. Some of these pairs are needed to make the croquet hoops, which are formed by the couples facing each other with their arms in the air and hands touching but leaving enough space between their bodies for the 'ball' to pass through. The other pairs form the croquet ball (a blindfolded player) and the mallet (their partner). To win, the 'mallet' must direct his 'ball' through the hoops before any of the opponent teams. They move the ball by holding its shoulders, turning it in the intended direction, then setting it off. No directional commands are given except a shouted 'Stop'.

Teams take it in turns to play and the usual croquet rules apply. If you get your ball through a hoop you get another turn. If your ball hits an opponent's, they stay where they are, nursing their bruises, whilst you get another go.

Human Boules is similar in form to Human Croquet and is the perfect beach game, especially if you want to attract startled looks from other beach dwellers.

Split everyone bar one player into two teams. Each team is formed of one 'thrower' with the rest forming the boules – these players are all blindfolded. The solitary player forms the 'jack' and stands himself a good distance away down the beach.

Now to the bowling. Each thrower takes it in turn to spin one of his blindfolded boules around a set number of times and then, holding them by the shoulders, faces them in the required direction and tells them the number of steps to take.

The boule must obey as best they can. Obviously the thrower must be skilled in judging the length of individual players' steps and also the dizzy curve they will have acquired from spinning around. Points are gained for the player who gets their boules nearest to the 'jack'.

To play **Human Curling** a little more equipment, as well as an ice rink, is needed. The curling stones are created by attaching the inner tube of a tractor tyre to a smooth baseboard. Players (wearing crash helmets) sprint along the ice, dive face forwards onto the inner tube, and with their acquired momentum go hurtling towards the target. The player that gets nearest wins.

Gasing – Competitive Top Spinning

Children have played with spinning tops for hundreds of years – they are probably the oldest recorded toy – but on the east coast of Malaysia they have made spinning tops into something approaching an art form with the game of **Gasing**.

The spinning tops (Gasing, in Malay) are superb hand-crafted hardwood and lead creations. Each individually named Gasing measures up to 25cm in diameter and weighs a hefty 2.7–3.6kg. The throwers (*tukang gasing*) tightly wind a 5m rope to the top, loop one end around their wrist and throw it at a 90cm-square clay platform, where it is scooped up by the catch man onto a wooden paddle. This paddle is lubricated with coconut oil to aid in the length of the top's spin. Teams, consisting of up to forty people (throwers, makers and catchers), set their tops spinning at the same time and it is the longest spin that wins. A good length spin is a staggering one and a half hours. An excellent spin lasts an almost unbelievable two hours.

Top competitions between teams, watched by hundreds of spectators, consist of five rounds and last most of the day.

Human Caterpillar Track Racing

Human Caterpillar Track Racing is a great way to reuse the box your washing machine came in whilst shedding a few excess pounds and squashing a few friends.

Get the largest cardboard box possible and tear off all the top and bottom flaps. What you are left with is the four sides, which, if creased further times, can be made into something resembling the caterpillar track you would see on a tank or mechanical digger. Now, with the box on its side, players lie down next to each other inside it (for the game to work well they need to be fairly tightly packed). By turning their bodies in unison, like human wheels, players can now move the box forwards. Often beginners tend to rotate at different speeds, causing a crushing of neighbouring players and an overall lack of motion, but once they get synchronised it is a wonderful sight to see the cardboard track moving off at speed.

Fastest over the course, wins.

Aunt Sally, Kubb and Gorodki

Aunt Sally is a skittles game that is played almost exclusively in the pubs of Oxfordshire. It is believed to have been started by Royalist Soldiers in the English Civil War, although its true origin remains mysterious, with a few competing theories of its development. A particularly grizzly version is that Aunt Sally was derived from a game where a live chicken was tied to a stake with players throwing clubs at it.

Today, the game consists of a single wooden target – known as the Doll. This is 15cm high and stands above the ground on a raised platform. Two teams of eight players are formed, and each player in turn throws six 45cm clubs, underarm, at the Doll from a distance of 9m. The total number of times the target is knocked over in the combined forty-eight throws is the team's score. Like Dwile Flunking, Aunt Sally has its own terminology, which includes a round being known as a 'Horse' and a player who misses the Doll being a 'Blobber'.

Kubb is an ancient Scandinavian version of skittles which is over 1,000 years old. Theories abound on its origin, but the most colourful, and therefore the most likely to be untrue, is that it was a game invented by Vikings using the skulls and leg bones of their victims. Over the years the popularity of the game declined, until 1995 when the World Championships in Gotland were created. The game is now extremely popular in Sweden and spreading rapidly worldwide.

Two teams of six play on a 52.5m by 85m pitch. In the centre is the King (a 30cm high wooden block) and at either end each team has five base Kubbs (15cm high wooden blocks). Team A takes their turn in throwing six wooden batons at their opponent's base Kubbs, and, if hit, these are then thrown by team B into team A's half and stood up where they land. Now team B must knock down these additional field Kubbs before attempting the base ones. And so it goes on until one team has knocked down all the Kubbs in their opponent's half of the field and can now make an attempt on the King, which if knocked over ends the game.

The Russian version of street skittles, **Gorodki** (Russian for 'little towns'), is a unique game that has been played for centuries but only got a standardised set of rules in the 1920s. The target skittles are five cylindrical wooden blocks (about 15cm in length) which are set up in a series of fifteen distinctive formations that represent Star, Gun, Sickle, Cannon, etc. These formations (the towns) are placed inside a chalked square area 13m away from the throwers who wield impressive 1m long, heavy wooden batons which they hurl aggressively at the skittles in a sideways throw. The aim is to knock all sticks in the town outside of their containing square. Once all skittles have been removed the next formation is set up. The team that takes the fewest throws to destroy all fifteen 'towns', wins.

Headstand Human Skittles

Headstand Human Skittles is a human skittles variation that is probably best played on the beach and requires only some footballs and a modest degree of gymnastic ability to play.

The skittles are formed by ideally nine players performing headstands on the sand. They should form the familiar skittles diamond formation and position themselves close enough together so that if one falls over they have a good chance of knocking over a neighbour or two. Also, the players should perform their headstands so that their backs are facing the two ball players. These two players now take it in turns to kick three soft footballs each into the group of skittles. Whoever knocks over the most skittles, wins.

Heels on Wheels Games

Human Go-kart is a bizarre group game that combines the thrill and danger of travelling in your home-built go-kart with a group trust-building exercise.

For teams of five players (four of which wear roller skates), players should stand in two pairs, one in front of the other, all facing the same direction and at the top of a slope. Players use their outside hands to hold onto the person either in front or behind them, and their inside hands to hold the adjacent person's hands. In this way they form a human cart. The fifth player is supported in this cart by lying horizontally with their legs and back supported by the joined hands. They can choose to travel feet first or, if they are feeling particularly brave, headfirst down the hill. Any player who is deemed to have either broken a hand grip or skated badly enough to make the cart collapse has to pilot it next time.

Guardians of the nation's children have already passed judgement on the popular Heelie (a training shoe with a small in-built wheel in the heel) claiming them to be a danger to health, posture and probably even a major contributor to global warming. Confuse and enrage these people even further by playing **Heelie Push** in the streets outside their houses. Players pair up: one heelie wearer with one in normal shoes. The heelie wearer leans back so that their partner is holding them under the arms and keeping their body stiff and their heel wheels on the ground, then they are pushed down the road as quickly as possible. This can be made even more fun if you can find a road with speed bumps.

The thrilling lack of control and coordination that is felt when you and a partner tie your adjacent legs together at the ankle is amplified if you are both wearing roller or in-line skates. For **Three-legged Roller Skate Racing** everyone pairs up, puts on their skates, ties their legs together, then races, usually quite carefully, to the finishing line. For a less extreme game – but one that is still quite entertaining – only wear a skate on the foot of the tied leg.

Conger Cuddling

Conger Cuddling is an outdoor version of Mangel-wurzel Skittles (see page 45) and has been played in Lyme Regis, Dorset, over the last thirty years. It is the same game except, instead of a root vegetable, a dead conger eel is used.

Ideally the eel should be about 1.5m in length (approximately 9kg in weight) and once again this is tied up on a rope and used to knock over human skittles. The eel has the advantage over the mangel-wurzel of being heavier and more slippery. Skittle teams play against each other to see which one can have the most men left standing.

Animal rights activists have recently threatened a national campaign and succeeded in stopping this marvellous game. In future, the eel will be replaced on the end of the rope by a buoy. That's B-U-O-Y – as in the plastic ball used at sea – at least, I hope it's that one…

Plant-pot Racing

For a perfect summer garden party you need the best garden games. **Plant-pot Racing** is a sort of scaled-up version of stilts, made from tin cans and string.

To play, you will need some old shoes and the largest plastic plant pots you can find. Simply turn a couple of pots upside down and attach the old shoes to the base of the pots either by using a staple gun or the liberal application of gaffer tape. A player can now slip his feet into his flowerpot shoes and get ready to race – although race is a misnomer as most players are quite cautious. Being strong headed in Plant-pot Racing usually leads to an undignified crash landing into the cold frame.

Piggy Back Games

Playing **Piggy Backs** has formed a major part of childhood games since the Romans invaded Britain in 55BC on, incredibly enough, piggy back and defeated the Anglo-Saxons, who were yet to discover it. And there are many great games to be had from this porcine formation.

Piggy Back Fighting (each rider aims to pull over a competing rider) and **Piggy Back Racing** (fastest over a course – include jumps and water obstacles for greater fun) are both very well-known versions of pig-type fun. However, it is **Piggy Back Polo** in particular that deserves to be more widely played. Excellent in the garden after a few ginger beers, Piggy Back Polo is an energetic and immensely entertaining game.

Pair up the players – one large and one small. (Teams of three or more piggies work well.) Use jumpers to make the goals and for the ball use something large, such as a light football or beach ball. Each rider is then given a hockey stick and the game starts. The fun comes from producing a penetrating through pass or dribbling past defenders rather than illegal moves such as knocking off a fellow jockey and giving them concussion.

If fighting is still of interest, instead of Piggies one can try **Horse Fighting**. To make a horse (a slightly more realistic creation than a piggy) you need three players. One player bends down behind another and grabs them around the waist, in the same formation as for a pantomime horse, while a third player, the jockey, sits on their back. Fighting being the obvious next step in this game, players form as many horses as possible and try to knock each other over using brute force. Or you can get some foam rubber poles and have a jousting tournament.

The Japanese are keen piggy–back fighters in a popular game that they call **Kibasen** (Cavalry Battle). Kibasen is for teams of four players. Three people stand in a triangular formation, facing the same way, and hold hands. This enables the fourth member to perch on the back of the front player with his feet supported by the others' hands. All riders wear a hat or headband. Now, battle commences. The aim is for each group to charge towards the other and for the rider to grab and remove an opponent rider's hat, thus eliminating that team from the game. Games can be simply between two teams of four or, as often happens, the whole school forms two armies and a full-scale Kibasen battle is held.

A note should be made here of the obscure Victorian street game of **Piggy Back Swimming**. Get all players into teams of two; one member of each pair bends over, holding their hands behind their knees. The other players now lie, stomach down, crossways across their backs and simultaneously perform the swimming strokes of their choice. The team that lasts the longest, without the swimmer falling off or the piggy collapsing, wins.

If you want to be really daring, go for backstroke.

Rhubarb Racing and Rhubarb Thrashing

An elementary, brutal garden game, **Rhubarb Racing** is three-legged racing's minacious cousin.

Players are grouped into teams of three or more. Generally, the bigger the groups the more chaotic the race will be. Each group is now tightly bound together with a long rope, much like sticks of rhubarb. Then the groups race against each other over a set distance.

For more fun, each team should shout 'rhubarb' as they run, and spectators can shout 'crumble' when a team collapses in an undignified heap.

A pub game that has languished in obscurity and has been shrouded in mystery for so long that it probably doesn't exist, **Rhubarb Thrashing** may well be the result of a fevered and drunken imagination. If so, then perhaps now is the time to start playing this marvellous game for real.

To play Rhubarb Thrashing requires only some dustbins, blindfolds, and a generous selection of freshly picked rhubarb sticks. Two empty dustbins, without lids, are placed facing each other. One player climbs into each of the dustbins and they put on their blindfolds. The two then proceed to try to hit each other around the head with their sticks of rhubarb. The winner is decided by one fall or a submission. There has been much debate about whether the rhubarb leaves should be left on (rhubarb leaves are poisonous, after all, so this could make the game dangerous) and also about whether players should take it in turns to strike or just wildly thrash at each other. Either way, a brilliant pub game; a treat for competitors and spectators alike.

One Man and His Dog and Robots

One Man and His Dog is the perfect garden game in which to practise your whistling – to say nothing of your Welsh hill-farmer impersonation skills.

Pair up players: one 'farmer' and one 'dog'. Everyone helps to set up a course which can contain gates (two jumpers on the ground), an agility part such as a weaving (bamboo canes pushed into the ground), and jumps (raised planks of wood).

The farmers then blindfold their partners/dogs and each dog must now be guided through the course by the farmer's shouts and whistles as quickly and accurately as possible. For greater authenticity, the dogs can be given names and made to complete the course on all fours. The team that completes the course in the quickest time, wins.

Robots is similar in form to One Man and His Dog, except that here blindfolded players must walk in a jerky, robotic fashion around a course, directed verbally by a seeing player. One other difference is that all teams compete at once, causing confusion and hilarity as robots get confused by competitors' instructions, crash into each other and fall over.

Samurai

The generally correct assumption that video games encourage square-eyed, lardy kids with limited social skills can be fixed if you make these games more active by getting the children to play real-life simulations of them. **Samurai** is one such game.

Players are paired up, one being the 'fighter', the other their 'controller'. The warriors are blindfolded and then armed with their swords – rolled-up and taped newspapers – and stand in the centre of the room facing each other, a small distance apart. Their controllers simultaneously shout instructions such as step forward, left turn, body blow, head strike, etc. (as if they were controlling a character in a video game), the aim being to land blows on delicate areas of the opposition. Confusion and violence ensue. Points can be awarded for various parts of the body hit.

Spit Racing

If you are looking for an extremely unusual game that combines athleticism and stupidity with possible hygiene issues, you need look no further than **Spit Racing**.

The simple (and disgusting) idea is that players race against each other by spitting saliva as far forward as possible, then rushing to the point where it hits the ground. Then they must spit again, and so on until someone reaches the finishing line first and is declared the winner.

Obviously, a combination of solid running and spitting ability is required to be good at the game. A good time for the 100m would be about ninety seconds, although times improve dramatically if there is a strong following wind. Remember, never play into a head wind.

Split the Kipper

Split the Kipper, incredibly, was a popular game played by children in the 1970s.

All that is required to play it is soft ground, stout shoes, a knife, and large amounts of stupidity. That's right, a game for children involving knives.

Two players stand opposite each other at a distance of 1 or 2 metres with their legs together. The leading player, the one with the knife, then aims and throws

their weapon so that it lands close to, but outside, their opponent's feet. The striking of any part of the opponent's body causes the thrower to lose, although this may be of little consolation to the victor. If the knife is deemed too far away, or if it doesn't stick in the ground at all, it is a 'no throw' and doesn't count, and it then becomes the second player's turn. If it is a good throw, the second player has to move his nearest foot to where the knife landed. It is now their turn to throw back in the same way.

The game continues with each player taking turns to throw the knife whilst all the time trying to remain standing, their legs getting further and further apart. If a player falls over, can't make a required stretch, or hits their opponent with a throw, they lose.

Once, and only once, during a game, when a player feels they can't take it any longer, they may decide to 'split the kipper'. This is when they can aim the knife to land between their opponent's feet, and if they achieve this they may now close their own legs to the starting position and the game continues.

Spectacular Deaths

Although it can be played anywhere with soft ground, the perfect environment for **Spectacular Deaths** is the sand dune.

The premise of the game is simple: one must die in response to the other player's imaginary gunfire, and the death must be as spectacular as possible. This leads to much clutching of chests, falling backwards off the tops of dunes, jerking your body in response to machine gun fire and perfecting the head snap whiplash response to the superbly accurate hit man hiding behind the pampas grass. Once one has mastered all these spectacular deaths, there is the ultimate dune death of the hand grenade lobbed into the sand bunker: a leap through the air with forward somersault to land triumphant (and dead) on your back.

The 'winner' (if there is such a thing) of the game is decided not just by who can die in the most sensational or realistic way, but who can 'remain dead' the best when the firer walks among them and casually prods the bodies with their feet.

Strange Swingball Variations

Like all blindfolded versions of normal sports and games (blindfolded driving, blindfolded football), **Blind Swingball** is both inspired, stupid, and often painful.

Make up teams of two players; in each team one person is blindfolded and given a racket, while the other is their 'eyes', telling them when to hit and whether to raise or lower their aim. The only other thing you need in order to play the game is a standard garden Swingball set. When you first start playing the game it is often the player that hits first that wins, the other not making a strike; but with practice this will change and exciting games can be had.

Space Hopper Swingball, like Blind Swingball, is a game that is almost entirely described by its title. Both players must bounce on a space hopper, holding on with one hand whilst they try to hit the Swingball tennis ball with the other. The minimal rules are that players must make at least one bounce per strike. The joy in the game is in hitting the ball high so that your opponent has to make larger and more daring bounces to reach the ball.

The other good use of a Space Hopper is to play **Death Ball**. This game is for two players at a time; one player holds a large space hopper (or, even better, one of those large inflatable gymnastic exercise balls) at chest height. Ideally the ball should be of a size that makes it quite difficult for the holding player to cling on to. The opponent is ball-less and stands a good distance away (the distance being decided upon by both players). Then, on a signal, both run at each other as fast as they dare. When they hit each other the ball between them cushions any blow but should fire both players backwards with some force. Any player that ends up on their back, loses. The victor, if one exists, gets to hold the ball next time.

Tissue Paper Laserquest

A fun summer garden game that is a delightful update of cops and robbers.

In **Tissue Paper Laserquest**, team members cut out small 'target' discs of tissue paper which they attach to the front of their shirts using safety pins. Each team member is given a large water pistol, or Super Soaker, and a container of back-up water. Teams separate to each end of the garden and then battle commences. A large garden or outdoor area with lots of cover and variety of terrain is ideal.

Players must attempt to soak members of the opposing team. Any player whose tissue disc becomes fully soaked is 'dead' and drops out of the game. Play continues until only one player remains.

To see this game in action is marvellous; with players adopting various battle styles from all-out aggression (rarely a winning strategy), well-thought-out team tactics with forward scouts, to the lone hitman hiding in the hydrangeas.

Remember to count all the players at the end to make sure that there is not one poor soul hiding at the back of the herbaceous border who, like a World War II Japanese jungle fighter, doesn't realise that the battle is over.

Trampoline Racing

It used to be rare to see a trampoline in someone's back garden, but these days it seems almost the norm for any household with children to have a large circular tramp. And if, as a neighborhood, you can get together and pool your trampolines, you can have a superb game.

Trampoline Racing is played by getting as many trampolines as possible and positioning them next to each other in a long line – at least five or six (but if you can get more, even better) should be placed tightly together. Players now take it in turns to race; this is done by bouncing vertically up and down on the first tramp and then, when you think you have enough height to start, bouncing forward. The idea is to travel along the line in the fastest time possible, but bouncing once and once only on each subsequent trampoline – a little like a human bouncing bomb.

Vitamin C High Noon

Who are you going to be – Marshall Will Kane or Killer Frank Miller?

Vitamin C High Noon is not, like the film, a metaphor about the perils of McCarthyism, but is instead a superb summer garden game.

For two players; each attaches an effervescent Vitamin C tablet to the middle of their forehead. These are the large, high-strength, 1,000mg tablets that come in a tube of twenty and dissolve readily in water. They can be easily secured onto the forehead using some strong double-sided adhesive tape, or even just held in place by one hand. Each player is given a full water pistol or Super Soaker.

Now, battle commences. Stand a few metres apart, face each other, and prepare to draw your pistol. You aren't allowed to hide or dodge your opponent's fire, you must stand your ground like a man. The winner is simply the first person to fully dissolve the other's tablet.

For variety, try playing the more tactical three-way shoot out – **Vitamin C – The Good, The Bad and The Ugly**.

What other game can you play that costs virtually nothing and prevents scurvy?

URBAN GAMES

Just because you live in the city and have no outdoor space doesn't mean you are excluded from the fun. You may not have a ready supply of rhubarb or drivelling sticks, but you can still play an urban game or two.

Urban Man Hunt

This is a street version of Hide and Seek. The most basic version of the game is where one player, the Man Hunter, seeks all the players (Fugitives) in an urban setting. Players wear armbands to distinguish themselves from 'normal' members of the public and are caught either visually or by tagging. Once caught, it is usual for the Fugitive to change sides and aid the Man Hunter. As with most urban games, players must remain outside and not enter buildings or cars. Playing with players that are not necessarily known to each other before or playing the game at night adds to the excitement.

Urban Man Hunt appears to have started in Canada and is now played in cities around the world.

Shoot Me If You Can

Shoot Me If You Can is an urban hunting game which uses the technology of mobile phones to replace a gun. It is currently played in Seoul, South Korea.

Two teams of players, each armed with a camera mobile phone, are given a brightly coloured T-shirt to wear which has their mobile phone number emblazoned on both the front and back in a large font. Play is contained within a designated number of city blocks, outside which no player can go, and players must also remain on the street at all times. The objective of each player is to use their phone to take a photograph of an opposing team member. Once taken, this picture must be sent to the game's controller who then texts the victim a message stating that they have been 'killed' and can play no further role in the game. Obviously, players need to eliminate as many opposition players as possible whilst watching their own backs.

Games are played both individually and with teams, which has the added advantage of tactical communication between players.

As the Shoot Me If You Can website said (no longer available)... 'builds consensual reality through mobile photography'. Quite!

Street Wars

If you have ever held a water pistol and fantasised about being a Jackal-like assassin, slipping through crowds unnoticed before clinically dispatching your victim, Street Wars is the game for you.

Street Wars is the brand name for an urban hunting game that is staged in various large cities around the world at different times. The game is designed to last three weeks and can be played by one hundred to one hundred and fifty people. Once players have signed up they are given an envelope containing their victim's details (name, work and home addresses, photo) and they have to wipe them out as quickly as possible. Obviously, every player is a target himself as well as being a hitman.

Players can hunt down and eliminate their victim any way they like, as long as it involves the use of a water-based weapon: water pistols, water bombs, even a glass of water. If you wet them, you kill them. On their death the victim must give the killer their own envelope, the person inside being the new target for the victorious player. If, however, the envelope contains your own details, you are a winner of the game.

The excitement of minutely planning a hit is amplified by the fact that while you are working out how to get into someone's place of work carrying a Super Soaker, someone else at that very moment may have you in their sights. And for up to three weeks, every time you are in a lift and the doors open you will feel the fear. Street Wars events have been staged in New York, Vancouver and London (see Internet Resources).

Urban Pacman

Many computer games are representations of the real world. New York University's Interactive Telecommunications graduate programme, however, decided to see what happens when you convert a computer world into a real-life one, and so **Pac Manhattan** was born.

Utilising a six by four block of Manhattan for the course, one player is dressed as the pacman and four others are dressed as the ghosts from the classic 80s arcade game – Pinky, Blinky, Inky and Clyde. Five other controlling players are also needed; these 'generals' sit together in a room and control one player each using a mobile phone. They can't actually see the players that they are controlling, but whenever a pacman or a ghost gets to a street intersection they must then report their position and the ghosts are told the pacman's state but NOT his position.

As in the computer game, the pacman's state can change when he eats one of the corner power-ups – these are imaginary but are fixed into position before the game starts by the generals. These provide the pacman with invincibility for two minutes so that he can then be directed to chase ghosts. If he catches one, that player has to return to the game's starting position before being able to chase again.

Points are awarded for the total distance the pacman achieves before being caught.

FESTIVALS

There is something to be said for the festival; whether it's a small, pub-based nettle-eating festival or a full-blown two-day event devoted solely to potatoes, there is always something to catch the eye, and in the case of The Redneck Festival that something will very likely be a cigarette from the Cigarette Flip.

Barrel Rolling

The tradition of Barrel Rolling has long existed around Europe, especially in areas associated with brewing beer. In most events of this type players race an empty beer barrel over a course, propelling it onwards using a stick.

The Flaming Tar Barrels in Ottery St Mary, Devon, is on a different level altogether – it is simply very strange. Here, on the 5 November, they race tar barrels that have been set alight.

There are a total of seventeen full-size barrels raced; these weigh at least 30kg, and when the tar is ignited the flames can reach up to 32m in height.

Members of teams race the burning tar barrels by carrying them on their shoulders until they buckle either under the weight or the heat. The next member of the team, often a member of the same family, then takes over and tries to make it across the finishing line.

There is also a women's race and even one for the children!

The event possibly dates back to the seventeenth century, but its origins remain unclear. One school of thought is that it began as a pagan ritual designed to cleanse the streets of evil spirits. You would have thought sprinkling some holy water about would suffice, rather than igniting barrels full of tar and racing with them.

Beer Barrel Chariot Racing

In Classical times the Romans held the Saturnalia festival to celebrate Saturn, the Roman God of Harvest. Now, every January, there is the Saturnalia Beer Festival in Llanwrtyd Wells, mid-Wales (home of all forms of Bog Snorkelling and the Man Versus Horse Race). The game highlight of the festival is 'Roman' **Beer Barrel Chariot Racing**; the sort of event that would have featured in Spartacus if it had been filmed in Wales and had been about beer.

The chariot is a metal beer barrel with its top removed and a pair of small go-kart-type wheels added to the base. The rider stands nervously within as a couple of bicycles with riders are attached to it. The teams then compete in pairs to try to achieve the fastest time around a figure of eight course through the streets of Llanwrtyd Wells.

Spamarama

Founded in 1976 in Austin, Texas, and held every year since, **Spamarama** is the Pythonesque festival dedicated solely to the prince of potted pork, Spam.

The main events celebrating Spam are the cooking and eating contests. Contributors vie to make the craziest edible creations, such as Spam Wedding Cakes, and in the eating contest they attempt to eat an impressive six whole tins in the fastest time.

There are also great Spam sporting events held in the appropriately named Spamalympics, which includes games such as Spam Relay (running with trays loaded with the tins), Spam Calling (a little like hog-calling but contestants must say Spam a lot) and some years, Tug-of-War over a pit of Spam. However, possibly best of all is **Spam Throwing**.

The Spam Throwing event is similar to egg throwing in that two contestants stand facing each other and throw a large piece of Spam between themselves. If successful, they move further apart and throw again. The couple that achieve the greatest distance without the meat breaking up are the winners.

Perhaps the UK can fight back if only someone would start the Fray Bentos Pie Frisbee Throw.

Bognor Birdman

The Greeks have Icarus, a myth about human desire and limitations; the good people of Bognor have the Birdmen – half-man, half-man-dressed-as-chicken – jumping off a pier for charity. At the **International Bognor Birdman** you will believe that a man can't fly.

The genuinely inspired idea of trying to fly by jumping off the end of a pier took hold in Selsey (on the south coast of England) in 1971. The initial idea was to award a £1,000 prize to anyone who could fly 40m or more. The event took off (so to speak), and after a move to Bognor (which has the added advantage of an even higher pier) the Bognor Birdman competition has grown until it is now commonplace for crowds of 25,000 people to watch competitors from around the world attempt to fly.

Serious entrants tend to be extreme sports enthusiasts with a penchant for hang-gliding who have decided to strap themselves to a giant wing and jump off a pier. Most, however, are doing it purely for the fun and the charity, adopting wonderful costumes and creations, often as birds, but just as likely to be dressed as a toilet.

Even Peter Pan and Mary Poppins have tried but failed to recreate their flying roles in films.

Today, if anyone flies 100m they will win £25,000. The current world record, set in 1992, stands at 89.2m.

Bog Snorkelling and Bike Bog Snorkelling

The 1980s brought us Yuppies, Duran Duran and leg warmers, but also, arguably, the greatest Welsh sport of all time: **Bog Snorkelling**.

Held every August Bank Holiday at the Waen Rhydd peat bog near Llanwrtyd Wells, the World Bog Snorkelling Championships attracts bog snorkelling greats from around the world. A 55m trench cut out of the naturally occuring peat bog fills with peaty water and forms the course. Competitors must don wet suits, goggles, snorkels and flippers and travel up and down the trench in the fastest time

possible. Competitors are completely submerged beneath the bog's fetid waters with only the tops of their heads and snorkels visible. The main rule is that no conventional swimming stroke can be used, so entrants have to use their flippers to propel themselves and their hands to crawl and pray to God that the life-guards will find them if they go under.

The current world record stands at 1 minute 35 seconds, set by a Marine and international swimmer.

Bog Snorkelling is also now an event in Ireland (surely its spiritual home) with a competition taking place at Peatlands Park, near Dungannon, in July.

Once you've swum through a bog, what challenge is left in the field of strange sports? **Mountain Bike Bog Snorkelling** is one possible answer. Begun in 2000, again in Llanwrtyd Wells, Bike Bog Snokelling involves filling your mountain bike frame with lead, filling tyres with water and putting on your wetsuit, goggles and snorkel. Now all you have to do is cycle back and forth along a 40m long peat bog trench. The trench is dug to be about 2m deep so that the water comes up to about eye level. Extra weights may be needed to avoid floating, which can cause you problems if you fall off your bike and find yourself dragged to the bottom of the bog.

If cycling your bike up to your nose in bog water is not mad enough, perhaps you need to get into the sport of **Underwater Cycle Racing**. Still at a fledgling stage as a sport, events have occurred in the US (on a sunken aircraft carrier) in New Zealand and in the UK. Underwater Cycle Racing is usually held at the bottom of a swimming pool and requires the wearing of sub-aqua gear, plus the bike needs to be perfectly weighted so that it doesn't float off and is not too heavy to pedal. The world's largest underwater race, involving nineteen competitors, was held in Guernsey in 2005.

Strange Games with Toilets

In America they use toilet seats as quoits at the Redneck Games, but unique to Australia is the game of racing toilets or, as they charmingly call it, the Dunny Derby.

A classy race, the **Australian Dunny Derby** takes place annually in September as part of Winton's Outback Festival in Queensland.

For a team of five players, as the race starts one person in the team must pull their trousers down to their ankles and dash as swiftly as possible to the dunny (the Australian slang for an outside toilet). This is a box within which a toilet has been installed, but no door. On the bottom of the box a pair of wheels and pulling handles have been added. Once the toilet jockey is on their seat the other four team members must pick up the handles and race the apparatus over a 250m long obstacle course. Bizarrely, the event is run just like a real horse race, with bookmakers and betting and presumably the odd doping scandal. The jockeys are even weighed before and after the event, although how they would have lost any weight by sitting on a toilet for 250m is open to speculation.

Recently this unusual game has started to catch on elsewhere in the world, particularly as a winter sport in Trakai, Lithuania. Here, the same-set up has been used – four players pulling a toilet jockey in a hut – but with the added complication of racing on a frozen lake.

Note should also be made here of **Motorised Toilet Racing**. These are toilet-sized and shaped mini-karts, they have four small wheels added, an engine and bicycle-style steering handles. Top speeds are modest, but when you are riding on a toilet the last thing you want to do is take a bend too quickly and tip it over.

Christmas Tree Games

The Finns can set up a competition or sport for almost anything: from Sauna Sitting to Mosquito Squashing, but one of their oddest is the **Getting a Christmas Tree World Championship**.

The event, started in 2005, now occurs annually in Pyhajoki. Teams are taken to a previously undisclosed area of forest (to avoid any cheating) and given a set time to search around, choose and chop down one tree – and one only. They are attempting the difficult task of getting the perfect tree. Entrants are judged by their peers, who take into account size, shape, branch density and presumably whether it is going to drop needles all over the floor.

Once you have competed in the tree-finding competition and celebrated Christmas, the logical next step is to have a **Christmas Tree Throwing** event. The Swedes have a tradition of throwing old Christmas trees out of the window on St Knut's day (twenty days after Christmas Day). To further celebrate this (and to promote their own advertising campaign) IKEA launched the first competitive tree throwing event in 2008 in Zurich. Called, appropriately, the Knut, entrants attempted to throw trees the furthest distance.

World Gurning Championships

An ancient tradition, dating back to the thirteenth century, **Gurning** is the Lake District's remarkable contribution to weird pastimes. The World Championships are held annually in September at the Egremont Crab Fayre (an event that includes Cumberland Wrestling as well as a greased pole climb to reach a leg of lamb).

To Gurn, you simply put your head through a horse collar and pull the most disgusting, funniest, odd face you can manage. Probably the only event where having false teeth to remove and having the ability to get your lower lip to cover your nose is considered an advantage.

There are competitions for men, women and children and the winners are decided by applause from the audience.

For the last seven years the men's event has been won by Tommy Mattinson, although he still has some way to go to beat his father, Gordon, who won ten times in the 1960s and 70s.

River Festivals – Messing About on the River Strange

Bathtub Racing is a quite common sport that began in British Columbia, but one of the greatest races is held in Dinant, Belgium, in August. In this event, over two hundred and fifty vessels race along the River Meuse; each boat must have at least one tin bathtub in its design somewhere and be powered by paddles.

Entrants make much effort dressing their vessels up as houses, planes, and in fact anything you can think of, and judges award prizes for design, novelty value and sometimes speed.

The British Bathtub Racing world has been thrown into chaos following the cancellation of the Adur Tub Race. After thirty years of racing real metal bathtubs along the local river, the charity event sailed their last in 2006 due to Health and Safety concerns.

The oddest Bathtub event, however, must surely be The **Nome Bathtub Race** in Alaska – for a start because it is held on land. Teams of four people push wheeled tin tubs containing the fifth member in a 100m dash along the main street. Each bathtub is filled with water at the start of the race and must have at least 45 litres left in it by the end to qualify.

Running for over sixty years, **The Great Knaresborough Bed Race** (held annually in Knaresborough, Yorkshire) is a combination of display and racing. Scores of oddly decorated wheeled beds are paraded through the town before being stripped of all padding for the race. Teams of six pushers, who should all be of one sex, race the beds and the bedsitter (who must be of opposite sex to the pushers) around the town, up and down steep streets and even make a river crossing – for which, obviously, the beds need to be able to float. A list of very sensible rules state that each bed must have a horn or hooter and that beds should be raced in the left-hand side of the road, except when overtaking.

The great vegetable sport of **Pumpkin Racing** is popping up everywhere now, but the earliest races were held at the Windsor (Nova Scotia) Pumpkin Festival in 1999. The giant pumpkins are hollowed out leaving a hole on the top side to enable a competitor to climb in and paddle half a mile across Lake Pesaquid. For speed merchants there is also a motorised race, where a small outboard motor is attached.

A combination of binge drinking and concerns over recycling led to the typically Australian event of the **Darwin Beer Can Regatta**. Begun in the 1970s as a response to the mountains of discarded beer cans in the town, the event is staged every July in Darwin. Competitors build boats, ranging from 1 to 12 metres in length, solely from beer cans (an empty can making an ideal flotation device, flattened ones can be formed into the hull). There are competitions for the best-looking boat, but the real event is the paddle-powered race in the harbour.

Among other activities at the regatta is the solely Australian Sport of **Thong Throwing**. The thongs in question are not of the underwear variety, rather they are the beach shoes with a thong that goes between your toes. The best technique is, obviously, a boomerang-style throw, and distances achieved are around the 30m mark.

Hare Pie Scrambling and Bottle Kicking

Hare Pie Scrambling and **Bottle Kicking** take place on Easter Monday in Hallaton, Leicestershire.

The day starts with a parade of the Hare Pie (beef is usually used these days rather than hare) and three small beer bottles through the village. At the village church the hare pie is broken up, along with some bread rolls, and there is a mad scramble for pieces.

After this a team of men from Hallaton gather on the hill outside the village to face the villagers from nearby Medbourne. One of the bottles is tossed into the air and pandemonium ensues. Hundreds of players (as many people as you like can play) scrum together to try to get control of the bottle and move it to their village. Any method, barring the use of punching and kicking other players, is acceptable. All three bottles are used so the first team to get two home, wins.

Hare Pie Scrambling and Bottle Kicking are believed to have originated in the Middle Ages and even continued during the Second World War when, because of the lack of men, the village women took a more prominent role in the games.

Henley-on-Todd Regatta

The Henley-on-Todd Regatta, loosely based on the Royal Henley Regatta, began over forty years ago in Alice Springs, Australia. Both events feature racing in boats of all different classes, though only one is staged without water. The Henley-on-Todd boat races take place on the deep, sandy, dry bed of the River Todd.

Competitors make their boats, without bottoms, and race by holding them at waist level and running along the riverbed with them. Races are run for coxless eights, fours, and even kayaks and yachts.

For people who like to paddle there are the Oxford Tub races. Here, small bath tubs with wheels attached are placed on specially laid tracks and players paddle as quickly as possible, using spades in the sand to propel themselves along. There is even a surf rescue event, where teams paddle their wheeled boards down the track to save the struggling swimmer then paddle them back to safety. If you haven't got your sea legs there are land events to try such as Sand Ski-ing (four players strapped to two planks of wood) and Sand Shovelling (a race to fill a large drum with sand using a beach spade).

The Regatta is held at the end of August every year, except in 1993 when it was cancelled because of flooding.

La Giostra del Maialetto - Italian Pig Jousting

A festival game that isn't jousting but did, unfortunately, use live pigs.

As part of the Saint Gaetano Festival in Lazio, Italy, the locals played a game involving pigs – **La Giostra del Maialetto**. The game originates from the time when an excise duty was charged on the number of boars a farmer had on his land.

Teams of four players are blindfolded and each player has a bell attached to their feet. The pig or boar also has a bell, attached to its neck. The objective of the event is for the players to try to strike the pig as many times as possible using soft-bristled brooms. The one who strikes it the most times, wins. However, due to the pro-fusion of bells and the mis-directions of the watching crowds, the pig is rarely hit. Instead, players spend most of their time chasing shadows and striking each other.

In recent years the game has not been played, for obvious reasons, but there has been a revival of it with a man dressed as a pig taking the lead role.

Nettle Eating

In 1986 two farmers in Dorset had an argument. It was not a particularly unusual happening, and one that, in normal circumstances, may have escalated to threats with shotguns and the odd slaughtered sheep. In this case, however, it led to the creation of one of the greatest strange-eating contests. The farmers were arguing over who had the longest nettles in their respective fields and one claimed, 'I will eat any nettle longer than mine'. The longest of their nettles was around 5m.

The **World Nettle Eating Championships** was thus born and the event now takes place annually at The Bottle Inn, Marshwood, Dorset. Competitors vie with each other to eat as many stalks of nettles as possible, all inside a one-hour time limit.

As with any game, there are rules: the nettles eaten have to be the ones supplied by the organisers – you can't bring your own. No mouth-numbing substances can be used, although as much beer as is required can be drunk to accompany the meal. (The technique for eating nettle leaves without stinging your mouth too badly, apparently, is to roll each leaf so that the spines end up on the inside.) And, most importantly, once eaten the nettle leaves must remain down.

The world record of the most nettles eaten was achieved at the event, a staggering 22m worth.

Potato Games

The only potato-related activity from childhood that most people remember is the counting out rhyme: 'One Potato, Two Potato, Three Potato, Four…' In America they have a whole festival devoted to the root vegetable.

The Potato Days Festival has been held in Barnesville, Minnesota (a major potato-growing region), since the 1930s. It's a two-day festival featuring intriguing events such as Peeling Contests, Mashed Potato Sculpturing, Potato Sack Fashion Show, and even a Miss Tator Tot Pageant. There are also two rather strange games.

Potato Car Racing involves making a car using a potato, axles and wheels, and then racing it against other potato cars by releasing it down a specially designed sloping track.

Potato Wrestling is exactly what it says on the tin. Two people at a time wrestle in a ring formed from hay bales and filled with mashed potato. Each match consists of two three-minute rounds. Perhaps even more bizarrely, it's not the only place it happens: there are also mashed potato wrestling events at Clark Potato Day, Maine Potato Blossom Day, and many more.

Currently no governing body exists to create a formalised set of rules, but surely it is only a matter of time.

Custard and Gravy Wrestling

Wrestling in Custard is a regular charity fund-raising event held by the Cardiff University Custard Wrestling Society. They hold knockout events where a small inflatable paddling pool is filled with custard from 200 sachets (about 200 litres of the stuff), then four players take off their footwear and attempt to be the last one standing in order to go through to the next round. All clothes are kept on whilst dignity is discarded.

The Northern sport of **Gravy Wrestling** was officially founded in September 2007 with the Gravy Wrestling World Championships being held at the Lancashire Festival of Food and Culture. They have a similar set-up to Custard Wrestling, but there are only two people in a large pool at once attempting to force the other to the ground. The event, sponsored by the Campaign for Real Gravy group (led by Brian Rey of the Fenwick Arms), even has gravy helpers on hand to periodically throw more of the sauce over wrestlers. They don't like it too dry.

Redneck Games

The Redneck Games take place annually in East Dublin, Georgia, in the USA. They were created in 1996 as a joke response to the way the media was reporting the Atlanta Olympic Games, with certain sections claiming they were the 'Redneck Olympics'. And so the true Redneck Games were born.

The whole event being an Olympic spoof, proceedings are kicked off by a runner carrying a propane Redneck torch and igniting the barbecue.

Then, the games proper get underway. These include such gems as Cigarette Flipping, Seed Spitting and Hubcap Hurling. They also have Toilet Seat Throwing, which is a scaled-up version of Horseshoe Quoits. Unfortunately, they have yet to start the 'Squeal like a Pig' competition.

If you aren't feeling very physical you can always compete in one of the more display-based competitions, such as The Big Hair Contest or the obligatory Wet T-Shirt Contest. And for children there is the Armpit Serenade, where they try to make a tune out of that great childhood activity Armpit Flatulence (cup one hand under your armpit, pump your arm up and down and try to get the output to sound like a U2 song. Not that difficult really).

The blue ribbon events, however, are Bobbing For Pig Trotters – basically apple bobbing but with raw pigs' trotters – and The Mud Pit Belly Flop, where competitors launch themselves belly first and with as much style as possible into a large muddy pit.

The winners receive trophies which are formed from a crushed beer can.

Snowball Fighting

Unsurprisingly, the simple pleasure of throwing a snowball at someone has been turned into a game with standardised rules and field definitions. **Snowball Fighting**, or **Yukigassen**, as it is called, originated in Japan in 1988. Since then it has snowballed, so to speak, and has been taken up by the Nordic countries, especially Finland where an annual two-day Yukigassen Festival is held in Kemijarvi.

Snowball Fighting is played by two teams of seven players on a 10m by 40m pitch which has a series of snow walls for hiding behind. Play consists of three sets of three minutes each, and during each set the team has a supply of just ninety snowballs. The snowballs are created before each game using a snowball-making machine – which ensures uniformity of size and density and prevents the childhood technique of adding a little ice to the finished ball.

Each team's home area contains a flag, and they must defend this whilst trying to capture their opponent's, and avoid being hit by a ball. If a player is hit, they are out for the whole of the set. A set is won by either capturing the flag or by having more players left on the pitch at the end of three minutes. If there is a tie, the team that used the fewest snowballs wins that set.

Surely there should be a push to get Yukigassen into the next Winter Olympics? At the very least as a demonstration sport.

Welsh Bunny Hopping

At Easter time every Strange Gamer finds themselves itching to buy masses of cotton wool and double-sided sticky tape, dress themselves up as a rabbit and hop down their local high street.

For the past few years the Welsh town of Llangollen has hosted the Easter **Welsh Bunny Hop**. Competitors of all ages and sizes don their rabbit costumes and hop madly through the centre of the town. Unfortunately, the organisers almost had to cancel this year's event, and any future activities, claiming that they cannot afford the cost of the public liability insurance. It's a sorry state of affairs when the common man and woman are denied the basic pleasures of being a bunny and making a fool of themselves. Fortunately, because of the general outcry from the rabbit-loving Welsh, the hop will continue.

There have been unconfirmed reports that in this year's hop a Mr Dai Evans from Glyndyfrdwy stumbled awkwardly outside Sayers and in a bizarre fall broke his leg so seriously that he had to be put down.

Wolverhampton Tough Guy Race

If you want to get involved in a really tough sport and test your body to breaking point, you need to head for Wolverhampton and enter the **Wolverhampton Tough Guy Race**, a race that makes the assault course on the Krypton Factor look like a trip to the kids' swings.

This charity race, which is staged twice a year (in January and July), is an army assault course on a massive scale and is infamous for the organiser stating that no one has ever properly completed it.

There are over fifteen gruelling stages and over 8 miles of running, jumping, climbing and crawling.

Highlight stages are a slalom (running up and down the area's steepest hill), Grand National-size jumps over hedges and ditches, gigantic army assault climbing obstacles, single rope bridges over nettles, jumps over fire, extensive underwater tunnels and belly crawls under strings of barbed wire. One of the most daunting stages is the Viet Cong-inspired tunnels – a network of disused sewerage pipes to navigate, some of which are dead ends. Think of the fun you can have there when you find yourself with nowhere to go and a group of frustrated body builders with something to prove backed up behind you.

When the race is eventually won, about one and three-quarter hours later, the winner never does a lap of honour.

World Worm Charming

They may be able to charm snakes to come out of a basket in India, but can they charm out 511 in just half an hour? And can they do this under the watchful eyes of Fred the Weatherman? I doubt it.

Worm Charming came of age in the early 1980s, when Tom Shufflebotham charmed the aforementioned 511 worms out of a field in Cheshire.

The International World Worm Charming Championship takes place annually in June/July in the playing fields of Willaston County Primary School – watched by a large crowd of people and thousands of fascinated local birds. Competitors come from around the world to challenge the highly skilled local worm charmers, who usually win.

Rules are simple – teams of up to three people are randomly allocated a 3m by 3m plot of turf. They are not allowed to water the ground but must charm the worms out in half an hour using only music and vibrations. The most common and productive method is to insert a garden fork into the ground and then vibrate it either by hand or by bowing it (a procedure known as 'twanging'). Unsuccessful methods include singing Celine Dion songs and playing the bongos, both methods seem to drive the worms further underground. If a competitor does not want to handle any emerging worms themselves they can appoint a second, known as a 'gillie', whose job is to gather up any worms charmed.

There are prizes for the most charmed and also for the heaviest single specimen (6.6g was the largest recorded in 1987).

Since Willaston led the way in the development of this activity, worm-charming events have come out of their holes elsewhere. Of particular merit is the Worm Charming Event in Blackawton near Dartmouth, Devon. Founded in 1986, the competition involves charming as many worms as possible out of 1 square metre of field in only 15 minutes. The record stands at 149.

PARTY GAMES

Ah, the children's party. The cheery delight on their faces as they find themselves gaffer-taped to the wall, and the grateful thanks of the parents as they pick up Tommy and drive him to the nearest accident and emergency department to have the bucket on his head removed. Here are some ideas for party games. Don't forget the jelly.

Three-legged French Blindman's Buff

A verbose name for a delightfully simple and must-play party game. **Three-legged French Blindman's Buff** is the perfect party game for children who don't mind the odd bruise or a mild case of concussion and have non-litigious parents.

Simply tie one person's hands together behind their back (sometimes known as the 'French Blindman'). The remaining players are paired up and have their adjacent legs bound together, as in a three-legged race. The French Blindman now has to try to tag one of the other players and, because their hands are bound behind them, this necessarily involves plenty of backwards running and spins and twists. Couple his awkward chasing motions with the chaotic scrambling from the three-legged men and you have carnage.

Bell Battle

Bell Battle is an excellent party game which forces players to consider the combination of violence and passivity that yields the best results. It is also very silly. Simply pair up all players – one large with one smaller. The stronger of the pair gives the smaller one a piggy back, then each rider is given a handbell to carry in one hand and a plastic sword to carry in the other. Working as a team, they now have to get their opponents to ring their bell without their own making a sound. Success usually involves delicate movement, balance and good timing.

The team whose bell is last to ring, wins.

Body Surfing

Ask one of today's teenagers if they have ever body surfed and no doubt they will tell you a tale of being held aloft by the hands of others in front of the stage at a Maniac Sumo gig. The party game **Body Surfing** is slightly more genteel, though no less fun.

Split people into two teams. Line up all but one of each team then get them to lie down on the floor on their backs. Make sure they are lined up but have about a body's width between them. The remaining player of each team then kneels at the start of the line and launches himself, arms outstretched, onto the first few bodies. These players must now turn, as one, in the right direction to propel the

surfer onto the next players, and so on down the line. When the surfer reaches the end they themselves must lie down and become part of the 'wave', and the person who was the first in the line now has their go at body surfing.
The first team to traverse the room, wins.

Brat Sack and Whatever

There are many Victorian parlour games based around guessing the identity of a hidden person. Various means from examining ankles to listening to them cough or impersonate animals are used; however, **Brat Sack** brings a more dynamic edge to these games.

Players are paired up. One member from each pair leaves the room whilst all the remaining players are given a large hessian sack to climb into, the top of which can be loosely tied. These sacks, with the players inside, are distributed evenly around the room. The other players are then introduced back into the room and the race is on for them to find their partners and release them from their sacks.

Another variation of a seek-your-partner parlour game is **Whatever**. Pair up the partygoers – the more the merrier. One person in each pair is taken out of the room and blindfolded. Their partner is then given a common word or short phrase (traditionally those in common parlance, such as 'whatever', 'minger', 'loser', that sort of thing) and told to pick a spot somewhere near the walls of the room.

The blindfolded partners are then brought back into the centre of the room, told their partner's words and released. They have to find their partners as quickly as possible. The partners call out their chosen word to guide them but they can only do so a maximum of three times.

Bucketheads

Most great party games need little more in terms of equipment than a ball, blindfold or balloon. **Bucketheads** is an hilarious yet asinine game, for two or more people, that only needs a humble plastic bucket.

Two players place an object on the floor, preferably somewhere near the edge of the room. The object needs to be anything that is easily recognisable, even when confused. Players then go to the centre of the room and each places a plastic bucket over their head. The bucket should act as a partial blindfold, enabling each player to see some but not much of the floor at their feet. It is also quite disorientating.

The players then hold hands and spin around a set number of times. The point of this is for them to further lose their bearings and a little of their balance, but not to be totally dizzy. The race is then on to find the object first.

As well as immense fun to play, Bucketheads is a brilliant game to watch. Observing your friends staggering wildly around the room, heads in buckets, crashing into each other and over soft furnishings as they race for the prize is a rare joy.

Chocolate Lottery

Chocolate Lottery is a trick confectionery lottery game where there is only one loser and the pleasure, if there is any, is in watching their reaction.

The simple ingredients needed to play are as many mini sweet bars as players, a syringe, and a jar of hot pepper sauce. The sweets used need to be small enough to be eaten in one or two bites and soft enough to be injected with the sauce without it being detectable by sight, so a sweet bar containing soft nougat or caramel would be ideal. While players avert their eyes, the organiser chooses one bar and injects it with a small quantity of the pepper sauce. All players, with glasses of water at the ready, choose a bar and consume it. Who will be the unlucky player? It could be you…

Deer Hunting

This is a good party game for two people at a time to play, with most of the fun being in the watching of it.

In **Deer Hunting**, two players are blindfolded and one is declared to be the 'hunter', the other the 'deer'. They are placed next to a round table so that their right hands touch its surface, but opposite each other and both facing in a clockwise direction. The aim of the game is for the hunter to catch the deer and the deer to escape, which it will do if it runs faster and catches up with the hunter. Players must keep one hand on the table at all times. A time limit of a minute or so should avoid too much exhaustion, and if the deer remains free after that time it is the victor and is released into the wild.

The wearing of fake antlers and the carrying of a toy gun all adds to the drama.

Dork

If you have ever had the sort of day where every person you have met is slow-witted and maladroit but you still feel like playing a game, **Dork** is the game for you. Dork is one of the most directionless, simple-minded games going.

Form teams of four or five players; one member of each team is chosen to be the 'Dork' and is given a minute to look at each team member's shoes – the idea being to memorise which shoes belong to which person. The Dorks then have a large upturned bucket placed on their heads. This acts (as in the game Bucketheads) as both a disorientating device and a partial blindfold. The Dorks should only be able to see a small area of the floor close to themselves. They are then taken to the centre of the room and spun around numerous times until quite dizzy. All other players scatter randomly around the room then remain fixed in their positions.

The aim of the game is for the Dorks to find and name all of their four team members as quickly as possible using only their limited available vision. The more teams that play, the better.

Grub Up!

Grub Up! is a great children's party game; in what other game do you find sweets and bray like a donkey?

To play, split the partygoers into teams of two. One team member is given the role of an easily imitated farm animal – dog, cow, chicken, etc. – while the other team member will be a farmer. The party host will have beforehand hidden copious quantities of sweets around the house and it is the animals' task to sniff them out. All the animals leave the room on hands and knees, and upon finding a sweet they must call for their farmers using only their animal voices. The farmer then has to find their animal as quickly as possible from its noises and collect the sweets. If two animals find the same stash it is the farmer that arrives first that gets them. The farmers then remain where they are and set their beasts off on another search.

Balloon Games

Balloons are a feature of every children's party, but they are rarely used to their best effect. Here are three top games to play with a balloon.

It's My Balloon Snot Yours is an excellent balloon party game, but may not be one to play if you are asthmatic or have a heavy cold. Each player is given a balloon and a competition begins to see who can blow theirs up in the quickest time. However, there is a catch because players can only use their noses to blow them up. The best technique is to stretch the balloon's neck over both nostrils, breathe in through the mouth whilst pinching nose and balloon tight, then snort forcefully into the balloon. The player that achieves the greatest inflation is given a pin and can then chase other players around the room and try to pop his balloon next to someone.

Water Balloon Throwing is the balloon version of egg throwing. Split the party into teams of two and give each pair a balloon that has been filled with water and tied shut. Teammates stand a few metres apart, facing each other, and one throws the balloon to the other. If caught successfully, players each take a step back and throw again. The team that achieves the greatest distance without spillage, wins.

All that is needed to play **Water Balloon Volleyball** is a badminton net and a good supply of water-filled balloons. This game is similar in form to normal volleyball, but in practice it is very different as players treat the ball with much more respect. Your team gets a point every time the balloon bursts in your opponents' half.

Two Games with Rolled-up Newspapers

Get Away is a game that contains an almost perfect balance of tension, exercise and violence.

All players stand in a large circle, facing inwards, with hands held behind their backs and eyes tightly closed. A game organiser walks around the outside of this circle holding a rolled-up newspaper – or some other suitable beating device. Choosing someone at random, the organiser places the rolled-up newspaper into the hands of a player. This player can now open their eyes and hit the player standing on their right (usually around the buttocks). The hit player must now run away anti-clockwise around the circle with the first player chasing them and trying to land more blows. The play stops when the running player returns to their place. Eyes are closed again and the play continues.

Another marvellously crazy game involving rolled-up newspapers is **Dangerous Dog**. One player gets down on all fours, the dog, and another is their master. They have to handle their dog by grabbing the back of that player's shirt. All the other players now taunt the dog by trying to hit him with rolled-up newspapers. The dog and owner fight back, and if the dog, who must remain in an all-fours position throughout the game, succeeds in touching any of the crowd with either arms or legs, that person has to become the new dog or perform a suitably horrendous forfeit.

Guide Dog Musical Chairs

Musical Chairs and Blindman's Buff have been pushed beyond the scope of this book by their ubiquity and dullness, but there is wonderful politically incorrect version of the two games combined that needs to be more widely played.

Guide Dog Musical Chairs is the perfect party game; it requires only chairs, blindfolds and the ability to bark. Pair up everyone into blindmen, wearing blindfolds, obviously, and guide dogs. Randomly arrange some chairs around the room, one fewer than the number of couples. Start the music and then when the music stops the guide dogs should guide their owner to an empty chair. The blindman must not hold the guide dog's hand but must try to maintain contact by using a hooked finger through a shirt collar or belt loop. If contact is lost, the dog must use its bark to attract the owner; the dogs cannot speak.

Once the guide dog gets its owner to a seat they sit down together, with the dog on its owner's knee. One couple is eliminated each round, a chair is removed and the game continues.

Human Fly

As I mentioned in my introduction, there appears to be a modern trend towards increasingly lavish children's parties – we are talking stretch limos, hiring of

pop-music beat combos, Nintendo DSs in the party bags, and more, all to make it an unforgettable experience. The fact is that all you need to spend to keep the kids entertained is a few pounds on some rolls of gaffer tape – then you can play **Human Fly**.

Split the players into groups of four or five. Give each group a high stool and some wall space. The teams select one of their number, the lightest is best, to sit on the stool with his back against the wall. They then proceed to tape them as firmly as possible to the wall using the gaffer tape supplied, taping them over their stomach, outstretched arms and legs. (It is best to avoid taping over areas of bare skin.) After a set time, the teams are stopped and the highlight of the game occurs – the stools are removed, leaving the players fixed to the wall. The team whose player is last to peel off, wins.

Human Seal Racing

The greatest childhood chants and games are often based upon real-life events and environments. Ring a Ring o' Roses' genesis in the years of the European Plague is well documented; less well known is the Great English chair shortage of 1673 that gave us Musical Chairs.

But one of the best strange games inspired by its environment is the Inuit game of **Human Seal Racing**. To play an easy version of the game, all players should lie stomach-down on the floor, then raise their upper bodies off the ground by placing their hands under their chest and extending their arms. They should now resemble a seal (and be in the yoga position of the Cobra). Now, maintaining this position and using only their arms to propel themselves, players race each other to the finishing line in a seal-like fashion.

To play a more authentic and harder game, each player should keep their body totally rigid whilst balancing on their toes and the knuckles of their fully extended arms. Players now 'hop' forward by bouncing their body up and down, which means that each time they land they do so on their knuckles. Rather than racing, it is probably better to see which player can travel the furthest distance.

It's not until you've tried it that you realise how much upper body strength you need to be successful at Seal Racing.

Human Maggot Racing

A simple but fun party game, **Human Maggot Racing** requires each participant to lie face-down on the floor, arms by their sides, inside a sleeping bag. Bags that have drawstrings at the top, enabling them to be tightly pulled in around the shoulders, are best – alternatively, use masking tape to tie up the sleeping bags around the player. Now, maggot-like, players squirm as quickly as possible towards the finishing line.

Three Messy Party Games

A wonderful and extremely messy party game is **Russian Egg Roulette**. Strikingly simple, six players choose an egg out of a basket. The majority of eggs have been hard boiled, however a minority (the proportions can be varied for different types of games) are fresh, uncooked eggs. The players must now each select an egg with which to play. One at a time, each player must now crack their chosen egg hard against their forehead in one go. It is perhaps the only time in your life you will see someone look so relieved to have a hard-boiled egg.

Modern Art is a delightful party game which only requires some paint, someone to pretend to be an artistic pseud, and a load of maggots. Each player is supplied with paper, some paint and a jar of maggots; his aim is to dip the maggots into various paints and then let them wriggle across the paper, creating a work of abstract art. The party organiser plays the role of art critic, flouncing between works and giving critiques and prizes for the most relevant pieces.

Champagne Roulette is an adult drinking game that does not require you to drink anything, although you may find a drink helps to anaesthetise the pain and embarrassment of losing.

All players stand in a circle facing inwards with their legs shoulder-width apart. The first player has a bottle of champagne from which the wire and foil have been removed. They shake the bottle for a count of two, tap the base of it twice on the floor, then stand it upright between their legs. They must now quickly squat over the primed bottle for a count of five. If they survive, the bottle is hurriedly passed on to the next player and the game continues with the bottle once again being shaken, tapped and squatted over. If they fail, they endure a small pain from the popped cork and a damp crotch for the rest of the evening.

Mafia

If you want a group party game where you can pretend to be a murderous, corrupt Sicilian, the game of **Mafia** is for you. Playing Mafia is a great way to see how well people lie and how good some people are at spotting the fibs. There are many variations on the game, but below is a description of it in its most basic form.

With twelve players, say, each picks from a shuffled deck of twelve playing cards. If a player picks a picture card, he is a member of the 'Mafia'; if he picks any other number, he is a 'Villager'. For twelve players a good mix is nine Villagers and three Mafia. No player should let any other know what role he is playing. A moderator can deal out the cards randomly and control the rest of the game.

The game occurs in two phases:

Nighttime: Everyone must close their eyes, then the moderator asks the Mafia only to open theirs. They must agree between themselves using non-verbal signals who they want to kill and communicate this to the moderator. The moderator now taps this person on the shoulder and turns their card face up.

Daytime: Everyone opens their eyes. The moderator tells the group who has died in the night – this person plays no further part in the game. Everyone now debates who should be lynched. Players have a set time to discuss, vote and lynch another player, who on death turns over his card to reveal whether he was a Villager or *mafiosi*.

Nighttime descends again and play continues in this fashion until all the Mafia are killed or the Mafia win (the number of Villagers must always be less than the number of Mafia).

Note: To detect if someone is lying, try to look for forced smiles, changing the subject, touching the nose, narrowing eyes, bottom shuffling, gaze avoidance and long meaningless lists.

Puppet Racing and Siamese Twin Racing

If you used to be enthralled by Gerry Anderson's *Thunderbirds* when you were young and want to relive those days (while at the same time looking slightly stupid), **Puppet Racing** may be just the party game for you.

Each player has a string tied to their left ankle and then to their left hand. This should be fixed so that their arms must be kept at shoulder height in front of their body for the string to be held taught. A second string now joins their right ankle to their right wrist in a similar fashion. To complete the 'puppet' a third string is now tied around one wrist, looped around the back of the person's head and tied to his other wrist. The best, and in fact the only, way they can now move is by simulating Scott, Alan, and the rest of the Tracy boys with a puppet-style walk. Tie everyone up and let them race to the finishing line. Remember not to leave them as puppets at the end of the part...

A similarly odd tied-up game is **Siamese Twin Racing**. Here players are paired up and stand back to back. Each pair is now bound at the wrists and at the ankles. Tied like this they must race to the end of the room and then, to make it fair to both players, they must return to the starting point without turning around so that each person has to move both forwards and backwards.

Slave Market

Slave Market is a 1950's party game that is so far off the scale of political incorrectness that it must surely be due to make a resurgence in a post-modern, ironic kind of way.

Divide the partygoers into 'slaves', an 'auctioneer', and the 'slave buyers'. Each buyer is given the same amount of money to begin with; the optimum amounts of money slave buyers and slaves may need to be discovered by trial and error, but £1 each for three buyers and twelve or more slaves are the sort of levels that work well. The auctioneer then lines up the slaves in front of the buyers and starts auctioning them off one by one.

The aim of the game is for the buyers to try to purchase the most slaves without becoming bankrupt. To win requires a lot of skill, as you need to bid for slaves but not be forced to spend too much and be left with no money and fewer slaves than other buyers. Once slaves are bought they can help their master in deciding on the amounts to bid.

When all slaves have been sold the game ends and the winner is the buyer with the most slaves or, if players are tied, the most remaining money. That team gets the prize, but one can also be awarded to the slave that gains the highest price – freedom, perhaps.

Surface Dives

Surface Dives is a reasonably well-known party game and one which, once played, becomes quite addictive.

Place an empty cereal box upright on the floor. Competitors then take turns to balance on one leg and pick up the box using only their teeth. No other limb must touch the floor or the box and they must remain on the one leg until they get the box, then they can return to an upright position.

For more advanced players there are a couple of options for making the game more interesting. After each round of the game a strip all around the top of the cereal box is torn off and the successful players get to go again. Or play **World's Strongest Man Surface Dives**, which is exactly the same game but in this version progressively heavier weights are placed inside the box.

Thieves and Mob Boss

Another blindfold game that has sadly declined in popularity, **Thieves** is probably the most fun you can have with just a blindfold, some handbells and a stick.

One player is blindfolded and sits on the floor in the centre of the circle with their treasure in front of them, but close by. The treasure can be anything, but items that make a noise when touched, such as a set of handbells, make the game better. The player has in his possession a stick or a rolled-up newspaper. The remaining players take it in turns to try to steal the treasure without being hit by the blind-folded man. If hit, a player must return the piece of treasure and drop out of the game. Play continues until all the blindman's treasure has been stolen or there are no thieves left.

There is an excellent Thieves variation called **Mob Boss**. This time, seat the blindman (the 'Mob Boss') on a swivel chair and place the bells at their feet. Now arm them with a couple of water pistols and cover the floor surrounding their chair with layers of bubblewrap. The idea, as before, is for players to approach the blindman, trying not to make too much noise over the bubblewrap, and steal one bit of treasure. However, this time they must do it before the Mob Boss swivels round and squirts you in the face with water.

This game works best if only one player at a time is allowed to make an attempt at theft. The joy in this version comes from seeing the increasingly paranoid Boss firing at the slightest noise as their treasure is slowly taken from them.

Trouser Ferret

Trouser Ferret is a euphemistically named indoor game that is a human version of the village fête game: Bash the Rat. In that game players attempt to hit a cuddly rat with a baseball bat after it has been dropped through a drainpipe, but in Trouser Ferret it is the players who get bashed – if unintentionally.

Players should be teamed up in twos. One player wears knee-length baggy shorts that have a hole in the lining of one pocket (already this game is sounding odd). With a hand in this pocket the player lets go of the 'ferret' (a sock filled with weights or sand would do) which then falls inside his shorts to appear outside at knee level. It is the job of his teammate to smash the ferret and trap it against his friend's leg between the knee and the ankle using a stick. No signals can be exchanged between players about when the ferret is to be released and the stick-wielding

player must hold their stick at least 30cm away from the leg. After ten attempts –
and many bruises – it becomes the turn of another team to wear the ferret
shorts, and play continues.

Warring Couples

Ice-breaking games used to be common at adult parties, especially in more straight-
laced times. **Warring Couples** is an example of a classic ice-breaking party game.

Players are paired up and have their legs tied together, as in a three-legged race, and stand with their adjacent arms over each other's shoulders. One player is given a dessertspoon to carry in their free hand. On a table at one end of the room is a pile of oranges. Strangely for a three-legged game, the objective for each player in the pair is different; the player with the spoon has to walk to the table, collect an orange with their spoon and return to the start. Their 'partner' must try to stop them, which they can do by using their free hand to knock the orange off the spoon or by stopping them picking one up in the first place. However, they must comply with any leg movement they make – they must walk wherever the partner wants to walk.

As can be imagined, pandemonium quickly ensues with players, oranges and spoons scattered all over the floor.

What Are We Shouting?

Everyone seems to be talking at once, it's giving you a headache – you can't stand it any more. Whatever you do, don't start playing the game of **What Are We Shouting?**

Everyone splits into two teams and then one decides upon a well-known phrase or line from a popular song – which should have the same or fewer words in it than the number of players in the team. Each player picks a word in the phrase then all players face the opposing team and shout out their words as loudly as possible and all at the same time. It is the opposing team's job to decipher the phrase, and if they are successful they get a point. Then it is their turn.

Good examples of phrases to use might be: 'Hit me baby one more time', or 'You know my hips don't lie'.

Wildebeest

If you want an animal-based blindfolded game for your party and find Pin the Tail on the Donkey a litle meek, the game of **Wildebeest** might be the perfect recommendation.

Decide on the number of 'Lions' that will work best for the size of room you are playing in and blindfold this number of players. All other participants will be the Wildebeest. A good ratio to have is five or more Wildebeest to each Lion. The Wildebeest must form a pack by making sure each is in contact with at least one other Wildebeest; this is achieved by holding hands or by grabbing a neighbour's shirt or belt. Upon a command the blindfolded lions are released and it is their role to 'bring down' a Wildebeest by touching it. Anyone caught leaves the herd, as does any straggling player that loses contact with the pack.

The game continues until only one Wildebeest is left.

PLAYGROUND GAMES

The playground is not always a charming venue for delightfully simple games watched over by benevolent dinner ladies; the playground is often a brutal place. As schools increasingly try to put a stop to almost any game being played that might result in a bruised arm or skinned knee, the nation's children will be allowed only to enter a playground wearing full body armour and clutching legal documents ready to sue any aggressor. Here are some games from simpler times.

British Bulldog

No book covering playground games can leave out **British Bulldog**: this is a game that is unneccessarily banned from many schools even though it is simply a version of tag (in the same way that Rollerball is just a variation of Piggy in the Middle).

To play, one person stands in the middle of the playground and all other players stand facing them, in a safe zone. They then have to cross from one end of the yard to the other without being caught. Being caught can mean just being held, being wrestled violently down to the floor, or having both feet lifted off the ground for a count of three. (Obviously, being overweight in this game is both an advantage and a disadvantage.) The caught player then joins the one in the middle and play continues.

The game involves many ripped clothes and bruised limbs, but most of all fun transpires whenever it is played.

High Jimmy Knacker

A playground game of uncertain origin, but it was definitely played in playgrounds in the 1960s and 70s. It goes under a variety of names but it is maybe best known as **High Jimmy Knacker**.

Two teams of players are selected – sizes of five to ten people work well. One team is selected to be the 'horse'. To do this the first player stands upright with their back against a wall and forms the head. The second team member faces them then bends so that the top of their head is against the leader's stomach and their arms go around his waist. Successive team members then join the line by adopting a similar position: a sort of rugby scrum with each player's head between the thighs of the player in front. In this way the human horse is created. It is now time for the action. One by one the opposing team must run and leapfrog over the tail of the horse, trying to land as far up towards the head as possible. Once they land on the backs they must remain in that position. The aim of the jumping team is to leapfrog all its members onto the horse and then hope the horse will break at some point. If that occurs the jumping team has won and it is their turn to jump again. If they fail to get all team members onto the horse they lose and form the horse themselves next time. If they all get on but the horse remains standing for one minute, they again lose and must form the next horse.

An excellent game that is both stupid and occasionally dangerous, but one that has been a source of constant employment for a generation of osteopaths.

Bok Bok

The South African game of **Bok Bok**, a game similar to High Jimmy Knacker, has been banned in the schools of that country more often than British Bulldog in Britain.

Two teams of four to six players work best. One team makes a 'back': a leading player stands up, the next bends over and holds them around the waist, and all others bend behind this one (heads through legs, arms around thighs in a sort of linear rugby-scrum effect). The 'back' can now move about as one while members of the opposing team take it in turns to run up and mount it. If by running around the 'back' the team succeeds in putting off a mounter who then fails to get on, they are deemed to have won. If they unsettle and dismount a rider before the whole of the opposing team get on, they have also won.

The mounting team win if they can get all their players seated on the 'back', or if the 'back' collapses or breaks apart.

Big Brother

Big Brother is all about brotherly love, staying true to your beliefs, trust in others – oh, yes, and violence.

Two players stand in the centre of the playground, one called Big and one called Small. It is Big's job to protect Small from the rest of the players; he does this by sheltering him, his arms around him. All the other players then try to attack Small whenever they get a chance. They try to pinch him, slap him and land a punch or two, and Small can do nothing to defend himself, relying solely on Big's protection. If, however, Big manages to tag any of the aggressors, they must become the next Small and pick their own protector, and then the game continues.

Combine Harvester

Combine Harvester is a variation of Red Rover (see page 136).

For two teams of six or so players each. One team lines up side by side and holds hands, but instead of just standing there they must now rotate their arms, like human windmills – this takes a little practice. Now all members of the opposing team run forwards and try to get themselves between the bodies without being hit by a windmilling arm. The windmill team can speed up or slow down but must not change their direction of rotation as they try to make contact.

Any player that gets hit must join the opposition, and the game continues until only one person is left.

Run the Gauntlet

Run the Gauntlet is a playground game that has been enjoyed since medieval times; it even features in the painting *Children's Games* by Bruegel. Today, it is usually played as a punishment for a player that has lost in another game, or maybe just for the hell of it.

All players but one line up facing a wall and then place their hands up high against it, forming a tunnel. The remaining player now has to scramble all the way through this human tunnel while everyone else attempts to kick him.

In Bruegel's time the game appears to differ, in that the group of players make two facing lines whilst sitting down on the ground, their feet touching. The single player then has to run as quickly as possible between the two lines as they attempt to trip him up and kick away his legs. Either way, lots of fun and bruises.

Human Space Invaders and Sitting Ducks

Here are two similar playground games that both involve firing a football at people.

A playground game from 1980's Britain, **Human Space Invaders** is that rare thing – a successful computer into real-life game conversion.

Line up a group of players against a wall, three or four rows deep. These players must shuffle from side to side, hopefully en masse, progressing only one step forward when they have shuffled a required sideways distance. The game player stands facing them about 15m or so away, armed with a collection of footballs. These are fired one at a time at the advancing hordes of invaders. Any player hit is killed and the game continues until all aliens are killed, or until one or more reaches the person firing.

Invading players can make the game more realistic by moving their arms from down by their sides to up above their heads as they shuffle around.

Sitting Ducks is the playground equivalent of the fairground game in which you must shoot moving ducks to win a prize.

The 'ducks' are created by players finding a playground wall and walking back and forth along it. The shooter stands 15m or so away from the wall with their supply of footballs and has a limited number of shots by which they must knock as many 'ducks' off the wall as possible. It adds a frisson of excitement to the game if the wall is of a reasonable height.

Joined-hands Games

Holding someone's hand is a sign of love, or at the very least friendship. In playground games, though, it is usually a precursor to a sprained wrist and grazed knees.

Red Rover is a commonly played and often banned playground game. Two evenly split teams stand in lines and face each other across the playground. Teams join hands and take it in turns to name a member of the opposition and call them over.

136

The person chosen must now attempt to break through the enemy line. Their reward for success is to return to their own team. Failure means they are absorbed into the enemy team. Either way, the game often results in plenty of fear and bruises.

Bullfighting is similar to Red Rover, except here all players join hands in a circle facing inwards. A sole member is chosen to be the bull, to stand in the centre of this circle and try to force their way out any way they like – but no kicking, punching or gouging from either side is allowed as the members of the circle try their utmost to stop the bull escaping.

If everyone is already standing in a circle holding hands you could always switch to playing **Crazy Daisy**. Here, everyone runs around as fast as possible while retaining their hand holds. Chaos usually results, with most if not all of the daisy chain crashing to the ground in an undignified heap.

In **Catch the Tail** everyone stands behind the leader in a line then grabs the person in front around the waist – as if they were about to do the conga. Instead, the head of the chain now attempts to catch the last person in the line and they obviously try to avoid capture. For double the fun, try playing with two chains at once, the objective of both leaders being to capture the other chain's tail.

Similarly mad is **Drags**. In this game everyone stands side by side holding hands and then sets off running until one end of the line decides to stop dead in their tracks. The rest should now carry on running around, which means that the players furthest away have to achieve super-human speed to remain upright. If no one falls, everyone ends up wrapping themselves around the first stopped player. Very quickly everyone should be tightly spooled up and the objective now is to remain standing – often an impossible task.

Tag Variations

Tag, or Tig, is a game that everyone is familiar with, however, there are a few tag variations that need to be better known.

Toilet Tag is a lavatorial version of the well-known Stuck-in-the-Mud.

Simply, a tagger is designated and all other players must run away to avoid being tagged. If a player is tagged they must adopt a toilet position by crouching down with knees fully bent and one arm held straight out to the side – representing the toilet's flush handle. Free players can then release this player by approaching them and pressing down on the handle and 'flushing the toilet', however, if they are tagged they become a toilet too. If any player has 'been to the toilet' three times it becomes their turn to be the tagger.

Bull Tag is an old variation that is rarely seen played today. In it the chaser becomes a bull by simply bending a little at the waist, making their index fingers into horns and placing their hands on the top of their head. As the bull they can now chase the other players, trying to jab them with one of their horns and hence give that person the chance to be the bull.

A much more exciting version can be played indoors in a smallish space such as a kitchen. In fact, a kitchen environment is ideal because not only do tea towels make excellent improvised matador capes, but the work surfaces can form safe zones where the bull cannot strike. So, players taunt the bull with tea towels or maybe slap the bull's behind before running and jumping onto a work surface to escape the bull's angry horns.

Further embellishment can come by simulating the role of the *Tercio de Banderillas* in Spanish bullfighting. Here, players attempt to attach clothing pegs or clips (bulldog clips, obviously) onto the bull's clothes without being gored.

Zombie Tag just requires a zombie to make it different from the original game. To make a Zombie, simply pair up two players (ones of similar sizes are best) then stand them side by side and bind their adjacent legs together. The binding must be more severe than in a three-legged race, where only ankles are tied; in Zombie Tag the legs must be tied together tightly from the ankle all the way up to the thigh, ensuring that the movement of the two players is sufficiently zombie-like. The rest of the players simply run away, screaming. Once two players are caught by the Zombie then they obviously (because of Zombie law) have to be made into a Zombie too. So their legs are tied up and the mayhem continues with ever-declining numbers of living players.

Urban Zombie Tag is an urban version of the familiar game. Play is best in a confined, limited sized environment but one that is public – so somewhere like the single floor of a busy department store is ideal. For a largish group of players, a set number are declared zombies and must walk around, zombie-like (arms out-stretched, vacant expression, etc.), trying to tag other players. The public element of urban games is what gives them their extra edge, with non-playing people interacting with the game either on purpose or unexpectedly. Once 'human' players are tagged they turn into zombies and the game continues until there is a sole survivor or the group as a whole is thrown out of the store by security.

Who's Got The Ball? is an ideal tag game for large numbers of players, but it does need to be played outside in long grass.

Split everyone into two teams in a central area. Everyone shuts their eyes and a non-player throws a tennis ball in any direction away from them. Everyone now opens their eyes and starts searching for the ball.

The objective is for one team to carry the ball back to the central area without being tagged. The game develops in two ways: either a solitary team member finds the ball and tries to sneak it surreptitiously back, or if they are spotted carrying it a tag game develops with the players passing it between team members, still trying to get it home, without the ball carrier being tagged.

Tree Huggers

All that is required to play **Tree Huggers** are two trees that are relatively close together and a group of four to twelve players.

Players should be split into two even teams and stand by their chosen tree. The object of the game is for one member of each group to hug their opponents' tree. If you are tagged by a member of the opposing team as you try to reach a tree you are 'out' and can play no further part in the game. However, you can only be tagged if you are nearer to your opponents' tree than your own. The game, played properly, develops into tense standoffs and daring dashes to tree-hug. Continue playing until a tree is hugged then all players re-enter the game for the next round.

Stupid Pranks

It is not recommended that any of the following games are actually played, unless you want to really annoy people, ruin friendships and possibly lose some teeth. However, they are fun. Inane, brainless, but fun.

Spider Monkey is either the height of stupidity in a playground game, or a hands-on insight into the life of primates. You decide.

In Spider Monkey a player picks an unsuspecting victim and gets behind them without being noticed. Then they jump onto their back and cling on firmly using both arms and legs and yelling 'spider monkey' or, if they wish, by just making monkey noises. The aim is for the unwitting host, realising they have a monkey on their back, to get it off as quickly as possible and before they crumple to the ground with the extra weight. The aim of the monkey is to cling on for dear life. People not directly involved in the game can make wagers about how long a particular monkey/host combination will last.

President is similar in oddity and dumbness, being a schoolyard game where, instead of one, a group of players ambush an unsuspecting victim. Pretending that there is a sniper about and that the victim is the president of the United States, players suddenly shout out, 'Get down, Mr President!' and jump on him, forcing him to the floor to protect him from the imaginary incoming bullets. That's all there is to the game, and for some reason the President is never grateful.

THROWING AND PROPULSION GAMES

The world of athletics field events appears to be stuck to just throwing discus, hammers and javelin. The real world has moved on with virtually anything that can be thrown being thrown. From mobile phones to cow poo, and especially food.

Spitting Games

Baseball is just rounders in drag, American football a confused version of rugby, but in Pit Spitting, America has created a truly great sport.

The International **Cherry Pit Spitting** Competition is held at the Tree-Mendus Fruit Farm in Eau Claire, Michigan. For thirty-three years competitors in various age groups have competed to spit a single cherry pit the greatest distance. The event is dominated by the Krause family, with Rick Krause and his son Brian vying for top position. In the 2006 competition Brian's children, Braden (nine) and Cole (four), even won their divisions.

The current world record stands at a staggering 28.5m by spit-meister Brian Krause.

Melon Pit Spitting occurs at the Watermelon Thump in Luling, Texas. The Thump (unfortunately not an event that involves fruit-based violence) is a four-day celebration of the locally produced melons. It features every melon-based activity you could wish for, but the highlight is the spit. The world record is just short of 21m. To see actual violence carried out on watermelons you need to go to the biennial Chinchilla Watermelon Festival in Australia where they hold a **Watermelon Headbutting** event. The world record was set here of forty fruit – and no heads – split open in one minute.

Strawberry Spitting is a featured event at the North Carolina Strawberry Festival. Unfortunately this game has not taken off at the home of the overpriced strawberry, Wimbledon, although once people realise how much they have just paid for them it is surprising that world records aren't broken.

Perhaps the most bizarre fruit- and seed-spitting game is held at the Avocado Festival in Fallbrook, California, where as well as having a race of little cars made from the fruit they also hold the world's only **Avocado Pit Spitting Tournament**. Holy guacamole!

The French devote a whole festival to the spitting of prune stones. **The Prune Pit Spitters Festival** takes place in Sainte-Livrade-sur-Lot (in the heart of the prune-growing region) at the end of July. Around one hundred people compete in the town centre.

Olive Seed Spitting is a possibly ancient activity that has had something of a resurgence in recent times. Events take place in Spain, New York and Australia. Players hold the seed in their mouths, take a short run up, then spit the pit accompanied by a whiplash head snap to gain greater distance. The Australian record is 18m.

The uniquely Australian game of **Dummy Spitting** (or Pacifier Projection, to give it its posh title) has its championships on Australia Day (26 January) on Whyalla Beach, South Australia. There are classes for men, women and children (who surely have some sort of advantage in this game).

Biscuit Throwing

The one biscuit you should never pick if you enter a dunking competition, the humble Rich Tea, is the very one chosen for its aerodynamic properties in **Biscuit Throwing**.

The **World Biscuit Throwing Championships**, an irregularly held charity event, were first held at the 2002 Glendale Show, Northumberland. Contestants had three attempts to propel a Rich Tea the furthest (the winning distance being an incredible 262m) in the hope of securing the trophy, a varnished Rich Tea biscuit. You can't help but feel the organisers have missed a trick here – if they included the Chocolate Eclair Javelin and Chelsea Bun Shot Put they would have the full complement of field throwing events in edible form.

For more competitive biscuit activity you should head to Slough in May. In 2008 the unique event of **Wagon Wheel Rolling** took place for the first time, at The Black Horse Pub. The game is a sort of biscuit bagatelle where the Wagon Wheels (large, circular, chocolate-covered marshmallow biscuits), are hand-rolled down a slope towards a scoring zone. Each player has five rolls of his biscuit to gain the greatest score.

Cow Poo Throwing

The humble cow is the basis for not one but three strange games: the mythical Cow Tipping Game, where you sneak up on a sleeping cow and push it over, the brilliant Cow Patty Bingo (see page 214), and the should-be Olympic sport of **Cow Poo Throwing**.

Cow poos (or cow chips, as the Americans fondly call them) are, once they have been dried, the perfect size and have exceptional aerodynamics that enable them

to be thrown great distances. Chips can be thrown in the style of a Frisbee or as an athletics discus, the main rule being that they must be fifteen centimetres or greater in diameter and if they break up in mid air it is the farthest-flung piece that wins. Further rules state that gloves cannot be worn, but to gain extra purchase on the dirty discus you may lick your fingers.

World championships are held annually in Beaver, Oklahoma, where the official world record of 55.5m was set. It is such a big deal in Beaver that their town's trademark is a cow chip wearing a crown, known as King Cow Chip. Another major chip-throwing event is at the Wisconsin State Cow Chip Throw. Here they even have an official song dedicated to the art of meadow muffin throwing: 'The Poop Scoopin' Boogie'.

An excellent day out, but maybe not the best event at which to be the official with the tape measure.

Egg Throwing

Egg Throwing is not just a pastime reserved for political protestors and youths heading for ASBOs, it is a serious sport.

The **World Egg Throwing Championships** are held at Thorpe Latimer, Lincolnshire, in June. Events include the two-person throw and catch, egg-speed relay and the egg-throwing with accuracy competition. Players come from around the world, with a New Zealand team winning the team event in 2006. Egg Throwing even has its own organising body: The World Egg Throwing Federation.

In the relay event, teams of twelve are spaced evenly over a 100m course. The object is to get a dozen eggs from one end of the line to the other in the quickest time possible. A time penalty is given for any dropped eggs.

In 'Throwing and Catching', teams of two stand 10m apart and throw an egg to each other. The distance between the players is increased by 1m with each successive, successful throw. If an egg is dropped that team retires from the competition. The greatest distance for an unbroken egg throw, wins. The world record was established in 1978 in Texas, when Johnie Dell Foley threw an egg the almost incredible distance of 98.51m to his cousin, Keith Thomas.

In the discipline 'Distance', the person who, obviously, throws an egg the greatest distance with it remaining intact, wins. In this game the egg is not caught but must land on grassy ground and remain unbroken.

Possibly the most ancient use of an egg for fun is **Medieval Egg Throwing**. Played in churches of the time at Easter, the priest would throw a hard-boiled egg to a choirboy who would then proceed to throw it to another, and so on – a kind of medieval version of Hot Potato. Whoever had the egg in their hands when the church bell rang the hour was the victor, and for his prize he got to keep the egg.

Haggis Hurling

Not many games have developed from the act of delivering a packed lunch; the great Scottish sport of **Haggis Hurling** is perhaps the only one. Apparently it began when the wives of peat cutters prepared their husbands' lunch of boiled haggis and then threw it to them over the ditches of peat bogs. The haggis was, no doubt, caught in the husbands' kilts.

In reality, Haggis Hurling is a modern sport invented in the 1970s as a spoof of Scottish culture which, after being played at the Gathering of the Clans, in Edinburgh, has spread around the world and is now played for real.

The haggis (a glorious mixture of sheep meat, oats and spices all wrapped up neatly in a sheep's intestine) needs to be thrown in a particular way. Contestants stand on the upturned half of a whisky barrel and must toss the haggis as far as possible. For the throw to be valid, the haggis must be edible and the hurler must not step off the barrel during the throw.

The world record was set in 1984 by Alan Pettigrew for throwing a 0.8kg haggis an incredible, astonishing 55m.

Mangel-wurzel Throwing

The spoof village game of **Mangel-wurzel Throwing** is what you would get if you mixed boules and strong cider.

A mangel-wurzel, or mangold, is a root vegetable of the beetroot family which is mainly used for feeding livestock. If this game actually happened, traditionally it would have been a West Country game that required skill, strength and cunning. Mangold Hurling has a well-developed set of rules. Players, who must be male and must also be bachelors, take it in turns to stand in a pitching basket and hurl a mangold over their shoulder at a mangold in a fixed position, called a Norman. The player that gets their mangold the closest to the Norman is declared the winner and gets to choose a fair maid of the village to be his Mangold Queen.

The joke, however, has become reality and Mangold Hurling has now begun in earnest. The inaugural throw was at the Sherston Scrump, in the small Wiltshire village of Sherston, when, in October 2006, men, women and children threw their mangolds at the Norman. Meticulous planning for the event involved organisers getting the villagers to grow mangolds from April onwards so that the event would have a great enough supply.

But prior to this event there are reports that a hurl also took place at the Three Counties Show, Malvern. No doubt after this auspicious beginning the game will now take off, causing a rocketing in the price of mangolds and a world shortage of Mangold Queens.

Mobile Phone Throwing

Considering the telephone was invented in 1876 and the mobile around 1980, it is surprising that it has been so long until someone decided to throw it competitively.

Unsurprisingly, it was in Finland (home to both Nokia and a predeliction for inventing crazy games) where **Mobile Phone Throwing**, the sport, was founded in 2000. Now well established there, championships are springing up in other locations around the world, including Germany, Holland, Denmark, and even the Ukraine.

The World Championships, held in Savonlinna in August, have various events from the basic furthest throw to team events and even 'freestyle', where it's not just distance but how stylishly you throw the phone that counts. The phones thrown are supplied by organisers and must be greater than 220g in weight, with competitors often having a choice of model to throw. The world record is an impressive 95m.

The UK championships, which have been running for a couple of years, are held in August at Tooting Bec athletic track and were set up to promote phone recycling.

Love your music, throw your Nokia!

Northern Throwing

They breed them tough up North, and when it comes to choosing something to throw they are not going to be satisfied with using a frozen pea or custard pie as a projectile; they prefer to throw congealed pigs' blood.

The Black Pudding Throwing Championships are held in the street outside the Royal Oak Pub in Ramsbottom, near Bury in Lancashire, in September. Pudding Throwing is similar to Mangel-wurzel and Haggis Throwing in that it is not entirely authentic and has a rich folklore heritage. Black Pudding Throwing is meant to have begun in the fifteenth century during the Wars of the Roses, when both sides ran out of ammunition and started throwing their local puddings at each other. Whatever its origins, Black Pudding Throwing is played by fixing a pudding plinth high up, 6m from the ground, on the outside wall of the pub. On this are placed six Yorkshire puddings. Players then have three underarm throws of the black pudding to dislodge as many Yorkshires as possible. The locally made puddings are wrapped up in ladies' tights to avoid too much break up and splatter in flight.

Welly Wanging is commonplace in village fairs around the world, but for an

alternative footwear throw you just need to head a few miles north from Ramsbottom to the village of Waterfoot. Here, in April and in the street outside the Roebuck Inn, competitors vie to become **World Clog Cobbing Champion**. Clog Cobbing, or throwing, is performed by standing with your back to the street and throwing a Lancashire wooden clog over your shoulder as far as possible. The world record distance is 28m.

Pea Throwing

Of all the vegetables that you can throw, surely the most unusual must be the humble pea. **The World Pea Throwing Championship**s are staged in a pub in Lewes, in Sussex, in October. The event is now into its eleventh year.

Contestants have three pea throws, or flicks, if they prefer, to achieve the greatest distance. The peas used are frozen peas and are supplied by the event coordinator; competitors are banned from bringing their own so as to eliminate the possibility of cheating by such nefarious means as injecting the peas to make them heavier.

The best method for achieving a good distance is by a straight overarm throw (you tend to look a little silly nestling a pea under your chin as you attempt the shot-putting method).

The current world record, held by Danny Tear, is for 38m.

Rolling Pin and Brick Throwing

Most towns are twinned with similar, or sometimes seemingly random, European towns. **Rolling Pin and Brick Throwing** is the only twinned strange game. In fact, it is not just a twinned game, it's more like quads.

Rolling Pin and Brick Throwing happens at the same time in July in Stroud in Gloucester, Stroud in Oklahoma and Strouds in Australia and Canada. The competition started when the Mayor of the US Stroud visited the UK town in 1960 and brought the game with him. The sport has continued ever since, with the Strouds in Australia and Ontario joining the competition later. Thus, competitors in the events are effectively competing not just with players where they are, but with all the others in the other Strouds.

Men compete in the Brick Throwing (world record around the 50m mark) and women in the slightly more feminine art of Rolling Pin Throwing.

Unfortunately, Stroud in Australia recently withdrew from the competition, leaving just the three Strouds to carry on.

Scottish Throwing

The Highland Games are well known to all, with Scotsmen in kilts throwing stones, cabers and hammers, but there is also a little-known Scottish Festival in, of all places, Hawaii.

The Hawaiian Scottish Festival takes place yearly in April and has been running for over twenty-five years. The events featured include all the throwing events associated with the Highland Games, but they also have a great subsection of games called The Scottish Housewife Games. This section comprises the superb Rolling Pin and Frying Pan Throwing. If that is not enough, they also have Accuracy Haggis Throwing – with the target being a frying pan – and the running of a mile whilst wearing traditional kilts.

Stone Skimming

This elegant game, played at least once by anybody who has been on a pebbly beach, is known by many names. To the British it is Skimming, to Americans, Skipping, whereas the Irish prefer Skiffing and the Danish, Smutting. The French, as stylish and contrary as ever, know it as 'Ricochet'.

Confusingly, there are two World Championships. **The World Stone Skimming Championships** take place in September on Easdale Island, Argyll. The main rule there is that the stone (Easdale slate only is used) must be no more than 7.5cm in diameter and must bounce off the water at least three times. The longest skim wins. The best throwing technique involves curling your index finger around the outside of the slate to impart the required spin, and then throwing the stone so that the trailing edge hits the water first. The current world record stands at 63m. The newly formed Wales Open Stone Skimming Championships began in 2007 at Castle Pond, Pembroke, and follows the rules set out above.

In the US, the **World Stone Skipping Championships** are organised by the North American Stone Skipping Association (or, NASSA – bringing stone skipping into the space age) and here the distance travelled over the water is irrelevant, rather it is the number of skips made by the stone that counts. The current world record stands at a staggering forty!

As the NASSA website says (see page 229): 'NASSA promotes stone skipping as both a natural non-competitive recreation and an internationally standardised competitive sport… a uniquely ancient activity that touches something very special in those participating'.

The same cannot be said about one of America's other strange sports, Cow Poo Throwing (see page 146).

More Things to Spit – Tobacco and Crickets

The American equivalent to the ubiquitous bounce a Ping-Pong ball into a glass jar game at the village fête is **Tobacco Spitting**. It is a staple of county fairs, especially in the tobacco-growing regions, with the World Championship being held in Rayleigh, Mississippi.

There are usually two events: distance and accuracy. In the latter, spitters aim at a target from a set distance. Often the target is on an old-fashioned, iron, pot–bellied stove so that a nice loud sizzling sound is heard when the spitter strikes.

The distance event is straightforward – the furthest wins. To increase their chances, competitors chew tobacco for up to an hour before spitting – it's important to get the right consistency of mouth juice; too thick and it's harder to propel, too thin and you end up with it dribbling down your chin. The unofficial world record is around the 8m mark.

Spitting Tobacco's urgh-factor pales, however, next to another American game: **Cricket Spitting**. Beginning in 1997 at Purdue University's Indiana Annual Bug Bowl, Cricket Spitting has grown and spread to other colleges in America. The crickets (Brown House Crickets) are dead when spat. In fact, rules dictate that the insect must be frozen and then thawed out before being placed in the mouth and spat out.

The world record, held by Dan Capps, is almost 8m. The Bug Bowl has plenty of other strange, entomological entertainments, including Cockroach Racing.

Food Fighting

From silent comedies to Tiswas, the fight food of choice is the custard pie. **The Custard Pie Throwing World Championships** are held in Maidstone, Kent. Here, two teams of four players each compete to fling flans as accurately and stylishly as possible into the faces of their opponents. Teams stand in front of their pie tables and only a metre or so from their intended targets. Each team member has five pies to throw at the opposition and judges score the event using a points system: six points for a pie to the face, three for one on the shoulders. Points are taken away for misses and there are even bonus points for originality of pie-throwing technique. It's a difficult event to judge because usually once the whistle is blown the game becomes a mass pie-for-all, which is over in a few seconds.

For the final, teams are given ten pies per man.

Hardcore fight fans should head for Bohemian Berlin, where possibly the ultimate fast-food fracas has happened in August/September of each year since 1998. **The Kreuzberg versus Friedrichshain Food Fight** is a totally wild, anarchic food fight involving hundreds of people on each side. The players from the Kreuzberg and Friedrichshain districts of the city congregate on the Oberbaum Bridge that separates them and fighting commences. Players wear head protection ranging from motorbike helmets, gas masks, or even the humble cardboard box and wield foam rubber truncheons and swords and food. A lot of food. They throw over-ripe fruit, eggs, bags of flour, rotting vegetables, but not hard fruit like apples or potatoes – that would be crazy. Fighting continues until one side is forced back or the police intervene.

If all this food fighting makes you thirsty, you need to visit Thailand. The Songkran Festival in Thailand in April is the background for the world's largest water fight. The three-day festival is dominated by massive on-the-hoof water fights involving pistols, Super Soakers and buckets, and thousands of locals and tourists. Anyone, including taxi drivers and police, is fair game.

Tomato Throwing

Tomato Throwing is the one vegetable-throwing event that is not about distance but is done purely for the joy of throwing over-ripe tomatoes at other people and, of course, getting covered yourself.

The Tomatina began in 1944 in the small town of Bunol, Valencia, and usually occurs on the last Wednesday of August. Interestingly, the tomato throwing doesn't begin until a large greased pole is climbed – a strange game in itself. Once the pole has been conquered, all hell breaks loose as tens of thousands of players spend the next hour pelting each other with five trucks' worth (100 metric tonnes) of over-ripe tomatoes.

The only rules in the anarchy are that the tomatoes must be squashed before being thrown and that only tomatoes are thrown (no stones, glass, bottles of ketchup, etc.).

After about an hour a flare is set off to halt proceedings and the council starts the clean up process by hosing down the streets.

Thoughts vary on how the festival started, with ideas ranging from it being a method of attacking local councillors, to people protesting against fascism.

Orange Throwing Festival

Ivrea, in Piedmont, Italy, can lay claim to the oldest fruit-throwing festival. **The Orange Throwing Festival** has been held for almost two hundred years, but its origin goes back to the twelfth century when the governor decreed that by law he should sleep with every new bride. One brave woman rebelled, killed him with a sword and paraded his head through the town, whereupon the locals followed suit, attacking the governor's troops with rocks. Replace the rocks with oranges and omit the decapitation bit and you have the modern event.

Ten thousand people form groups representing the districts of the town, dress in medieval costumes and throng the streets, throwing rotten and surplus-to-requirement oranges at a few 'leaders' who stand on the back of a truck, padded up and helmeted and try to return fire as much as possible.

Fish Flinging

The eel-obsessed town of Ely, Cambridgeshire, celebrates its slippery namesake in April every year with Eel Day. Eels are displayed, smoked and eaten, paraded through the streets as large papier-mâché models, and thrown. The fish in Ely's **Eel Throwing** are not real ones, rather they are sock-like creations filled with padding and weights. The throw is still in its formative years, so whether the best throwing method is underarm – as in wellie throwing – or a hammer-throwing spin is still to be decided. For real fish-flinging action you need to travel further afield.

The Tuna Tossing World Championship began in the early 1960s and occurs annually at the Tunarama Festival in Port Lincoln, Australia. Contestants simply

grab hold of a rope attached to a frozen 10kg tuna and, using whatever means they feel like, throw it as far as possible. Most people manage only a few metres, however the world record is an accomplished 37.23m, set by Australian hammer-thrower Sean Carlin. Other events include the 3kg Kingfish toss for children aged eleven to fifteen and, maybe most hilariously, there is the 'prawn toss' for little children. And to make sure it is all environmentally friendly, the tunas used are ones caught in nets that don't harm dolphins.

The Australians may be the best Tuna Tossers in the world, but when it comes to throwing Mullets, the Americans are the nation to beat. **Interstate Mullet Tossing** is a Pythonesque game that happens at the end of April on a beach on the Florida/Alabama border.

A 1.5lb mullet (the fish, not the hairstyle) is thrown by competitors from the Florida side of the state border into the Alabama side. Techniques vary, but the most effective one involves rolling the mullet into a ball and launching it with an overarm throw. Throws of around 45m are commonplace and all fish thrown are later cooked and eaten.

The exclusively French sport of **Winkle Spitting** occurs annually in Mogueriec, a small port on the Breton coast. Here, locals compete to spit the small mollusc the greatest distance. Winning distances tend to be modest, at around the 10m mark.

Typewriter Tossing

A great American strange game, **Typewriter Tossing** occurs in various locations on Administrative Professionals' Day in April (a day of celebration that used to be called Secretaries' Day).

A select band of administrative professionals are chosen to be hoisted one by one up to 15m into the air on a raised platform, an old typewriter in their hands. On the ground below is a painted target; the typewriter tossers must aim and fire their machine to try to hit the centre of it.

Fruitcake Tossing

It would be truly wonderful if America celebrated a National Fruitcake Day, but unfortunately they don't. Instead, the **Annual Fruitcake Toss** occurs in Manitou Springs, Colorado, in January.

Participants should supply their own fruitcakes, but one of the main rules states that the cake has to contain nuts, fruit and flour and mustn't contain anything inedible. As well as the manual tossing event they also hold **The Fruitcake Launch**, where cake is fired using competitors' mechanical devices, **The Fruitcake Hurl**, where the event's catapult is used' and **The Pneumatic Spud Gun Fruitcake Firing**. You get the feeling that they aren't that keen on fruitcakes in Colorado.

World Pea Shooting Championships

In ancient times it is believed that **Pea Shooting** was developed as a means for arable farmers to ward off the voracious lesser-spotted-cabbage moths from their tender young cabbage leaves.

Whatever its origin, Pea Shooting as an organised competitive sport began in 1971 at Witcham Village Fair, Cambridgeshire, as a fundraising activity. It proved to be so popular that it has grown to become the **World Pea Shooting Championships**.

Entrants from around the world compete against the legume-crazy locals for the fame and glory that winning the contest brings. In Pea Shooting it is accuracy rather than distance that is of importance, so competitors fire at a target 3.5m away. Only event-supplied peas can be blown, and the pea-tube can be no longer than 30cm in length. In recent years there have been reports of laser-aiming systems being used by some players to try to help them with their aim.

There is, as yet, no equivalent championship in the world of Spud-gun Shooting.

SPORTS

The creation of a strange sport is often brought about by the addition of a seemingly incompatible element to an already existing sport, such as a swamp to soccer, bicycles to polo and grease to pig wrestling.

Two German Games

The world's oldest, and more than likely only, **Cartwheeling Festival** takes place in Dusseldorf, Germany. The tradition of cartwheeling began there in 1288, presumably as a form of celebration when Dusseldorf was granted the rights of a town. Since 1928 the annual cartwheeling festival has taken place in the town's Königsallee (a boulevard in Dusseldorf) each year in May or June with up to 500 children taking part. There are two competitions: one for speed of cartwheeling, the other for style. Surely a British town should fight back with a Forward Roll Festival?

The greatest German strange winter game occurs in only one location and is very little known outside of it. The town of Little Neudorf in south-east Germany hosts the superbly named Arschleder Wettruscheln, or **The Arse-Leather Sledging Championships**. The game is believed to have developed here because miners at the town's silver mines used to wear Arschleder to protect their work trousers, but it is unclear whether they slid down a ski slope wearing them. Whatever, the competition was born in 1998 and takes place in February. Players compete to be the fastest down the slope, racing by the seat of their pants, literally. Hopefully, Arse-Leather Sledging, along with Snowball Fighting, will be a future highlight of the Winter Olympics.

Bicycle Polo

Bicycle Polo is a strange sport with an even stranger history. It started in India in around the 1890s as an offshoot from the standard horse-based game, increased in popularity and then flourished, especially in Europe, until the Second World War, when it declined or disappeared entirely except in France. In the 1990s the game made a massive recovery in popularity, with both the formal and various 'street' versions taking off around the world.

The game is played on a 100m by 150m pitch between teams of four players. As in horse polo, a game is split into four chukkers. Normal bikes can be used but shortened mallets are needed. In street versions of the game players often create their own mallets out of golf clubs, piping, or whatever they find to hand.

The rules are very similar to the horse version. Key rules are that players must keep their feet on the pedals at all times – if they drop them they must cycle off the pitch before coming back on. Players must play the ball from their right side and must have their bike positioned parallel to the sidelines before striking. The game is started with a bike joust; a player from each team rushes to be first onto the centre-placed ball.

No contact is allowed between players, unless you are playing an urban version of the game where often most rules are dropped and a freer game is played.
If you want more of a challenge the game to play is **Unicycle Polo**. Played mainly in the US, Unicycle Polo/Hockey is played as above with hockey sticks which, when not being used to hit the ball, are useful for making quick turns or just resting against.

Strange Football

A football match with a difference has been played in Bourton-on-the-Water, Gloucestershire, for seventy years now. On each August Bank Holiday, two teams of six play **River Football** in the River Windrush that runs through the town. The water in the river is only 25–30cm deep – almost knee height – with a gentle current, but still the extra effort needed keeps the length of the games to a reasonable fifteen minutes per half. It would be nice to report that the referee controls the match while dressed as a chicken and sat in an inflatable dinghy so as to represent an ancient pagan fertility symbol, but unfortunately he just runs around in the river too.

One of the great strange sports, **Swamp Soccer** was started by the Finnish in 1998 when the first championship was played. All you need for a perfect game of swamp soccer is a five-a-side-sized, badly drained piece of land and torrential rain before the game. Ideally the mud on the pitch should go from ankle to knee depth (in the penalty area). Teams of six play thirteen-minute halves along the same rules as standard football; except there is no off-side rule, teams can have unlimited substitutes, and all dead ball kicks are made by drop kicking. By the end of a good game all players should be an indistinguishable mud-brown in colour and be suffering from exhaustion.

Finland holds annual World Championships with over two hundred teams competing, the sport being particularly popular in Holland, Sweden, Russia and Scotland. The Scottish host the UK Championships at Dunoon in June.

Strange Games with Chairs

The humble office chair is adaptable to any number of unusual and entertaining office games, the most common of which is **Office Chair Racing**. There are two basic ways of chair racing: either team up into pairs and have one player pushing whilst the other sits tightly and screams, 'Slow down, we're going to hit that desk', or the purer game of one person per chair who propels themselves along as quickly as possible using their feet in the style of a sea lion.

Also of interest is **Office Chair Astronaut Training**. One player at a time sits in the hot seat and is spun around rapidly by workmates. The player lasting the longest or enduring the most spins, wins.

Office Chair Boules needs teams of two or more, in which one player launches chair-bound teammates. Who can get a workmate the closest to the filing cabinet?

Or you could try **Chair Ski Jump**. Position the chair between two desks and then, grabbing hold of them while sitting in the office chair, pull yourself backwards and forwards in the same manner as a ski jumper just about to launch themselves. Build up your momentum until you push off and go sailing across the office. The greatest distance wins.

In the US the chair of choice for weird games is the bar stool. The sport of **Bar Stool Racing** took off competitively in the 1980s. To enter you need to get a good quality bar stool, attach some go-kart wheels, a steering mechanism and an old lawn mower engine, and you are off. Fanatics have even built gas-powered bar stools and the more environmentally-friendly electric stools. As long as it's a bar stool, they are keen. The record speed for an electric-powered stool is a scary 45mph.

Hockern

Is it a sport, art, or maybe a dance? No, it's **Hockern**!

Germany's contribution to the world of odd games and sports is truly bizarre. Hockern (German for 'stools') is a little like competitive break dancing, only break dancing using a trendy 1970s-style stool.

Competitors stand in front of the Hockern judges and show off their best stool movements (sorry). These will include spinning the stool on the floor, balancing upon it (on knees, stomach, or even head), and tossing it into the air and speed sitting on it wherever it lands. One of the favourite moves is to make a high-speed throw over the shoulders, back through between the legs and then squat down onto it.

Another cool trick is to have a friend slide the stool along the floor towards you for you to sit down hard upon it as it reaches you. And it's not just a solo sport: there are synchronised group events too, that have to be seen to be believed. The superstars of this new sport are known as Hockstars and regular competitions, including the prestigious Hocktoberfest, are held in the nightclubs of Germany. Now is the time to grab your stool and live the dream because Hockern will surely be a demonstration sport, probably sponsored by IKEA, in the next Olympic Games.

Strange Games in Swimming Pools

Every British male of a certain age has purposefully ignored the 'No Bombing' signs posted on the swimming pool walls and has leapt into the pool in the fetal bombing position, aiming to create the largest disturbance possible. But it has taken the Germans to make bombing a World Championship. The Germans, maybe in a nod to political correctness, named it **Splashdiving** rather than bombing, although until recently it should be noted that the event was known as Arschbombe (literally, arse bombing).

In July 2007 the second **World Splashdiving World Cup** was held in Hamburg. There are two separate events that involve competitors jumping into a swimming pool from a height of 10m (off a diving board) or a scary 30m (from a crane). Entrants are scored by judges, with the highest points being awarded to the biggest splashes as well as supplementary points for style (somersaults, twists, etc.) and the ability of competitors not to let the pain show. Entrants can enter the water in the classic 'bomb' position, but the event is freestyle, with any entry

position allowed as long as the splash is large. As the official website so eloquently puts it: 'Splashdiving is to be seen as a community for girls, boys and especially freaks that have lots of fun at diving'.

In 2004 the Channel Five parody sports show, *International King of Sports*, featured the great water sport of **Association Bobbage** (alongside games such as backwards running, underwater shot put and longest skids). Players wearing swimwear and diving flippers take it in turns to make a standing jump into a swimming pool from a raised platform. The aim is to jump in and avoid getting your hair wet by the use of good feet positioning and by kicking your legs like mad once they are under water. Any player whose head goes below the water on entry is eliminated, the platform is then raised a notch and jumps resume until a victor is found. The record height achieved on the show was a remarkable 2.4m.

Underwater Swimming

Underwater Swimming is a bizarre sport that finally answers the question of whether a man will ever swim as fast as a dolphin. It is at its most popular in former Soviet Union countries.

All the usual length races are staged, with the difference being that the whole distances are swum underwater. Each competitor wears a large mono fin (imagine a pair of scuba-diving flippers fused together), making them look a little like a mermaid. The arms aren't used, rather the swimmer literally swims like a fish, swishing their legs as one, at incredible speeds while using a snorkel to breathe. This is sub-surface swimming; for the true underwater events competitors hold a small air bottle and wear a mask while they swim fully submerged.

The world record for the 50m is 15 seconds, compared with 21 seconds for more conventional swimming.

An earlier form of Underwater Swimming was trialled at the Paris Olympics in 1900. The competition was decided by who could swim the furthest underwater and remain underneath the longest. A Frenchman managed 60m in one minute. A famous Japanese entrant, Marine Boy, was barred from the event...

Brambles Cricket Match

Cricket is not the most easily understood game, but it could hardly be considered strange. **The Brambles Cricket Match**, however, is very odd.

The Brambles Sandbank appears out of the Solent (the stretch of water north of the Isle of Wight) once a year, usually at the end of August when the tide is at its lowest and when pressure and wind conditions are favourable. Then two teams of players from The Royal Southern Yacht Club and The Island Sailing Club rush, by boat, to the sandbank to play a game of cricket. The sandbank is tiny, only 200m long and in most places only 2.5cm above sea level. And, best of all, it is only visible for around forty minutes before the tide covers it for another twelve months. As it is submerged once again, players and spectators are forced back into their boats and head back to their clubhouses.

The game has been played for fifty years; spectators number around two hundred and fifty each year and during the game they even erect a temporary pub.

Cheese Rolling

Stilton Cheese Rolling, a twentieth-century version of a possibly ancient game, takes place on May Day in the Cambridgeshire village of Stilton. Teams of four players roll a Stilton-cheese-shaped wooden block down the main street in a knockout race against competitors. The only rule is that each member of the team must give the cheese at least one roll. And the prize for the victorious team? A whole Stilton cheese, of course.

Although it's a fun day out, Stilton Cheese Rolling pales next to the truly hardcore dairy game of Gloucestershire Cheese Rolling.

World reknowned and popular for spectators and competitors alike, **The Cheese Rolling** event has taken place annually in Gloucestershire for 200 years. Simple, fast, brutal, every May a large disc of cheese is rolled from the top of the very steep Cooper's Hill in Brockworth, and then competitors hurl themselves en masse down the hill after the cheese. The first person to the bottom, wins. The hill varies in gradient between 1 in 1 and 1 in 2, and has been described as 'so steep is it, that the rays of the sun rarely fall on the slope itself!' The cheese gets a one-second head start before the bodies come tumbling after it.

Injuries are common; there are a host of minor sprains but there are often some more serious ones, too. Occasionally spectators can also suffer and get hit by the cheese.

As a concession to competitor safety the event organisers clear the hill of nettles before the race. Surely they are missing a trick there – Naked Nettle Cheese Chasing anyone?

For a perfect accompanying game to cheese rolling you need to head to the Alsager Carnival, Cheshire, where the recently founded **World Oatcake Throwing Competition** is held. Oatcakes are thrown frisbee-style with the current record standing at 24m.

If you like the thought of following rolled food down slopes but the Gloucester Cheese Rolling is too extreme, the best place to start is with the **Totnes Orange Roll**. In Totnes, Devon, competitors annually chase their rolled oranges down the long, steep, central street. There are events for all age groups, culminating in the highlight where local policemen and women give chase to escaped jaffas. The event, organised by the town's Elizabethan Society, celebrates a visit to the town by Sir Francis Drake during which he gave an orange to a local boy.

Strange Chess – Aqua Chess and Chess Boxing

Although underwater chess (scuba gear and lead-weighted chess pieces) is occasionally played, **Aqua Chess** has a more novel approach to the art of sports combining.

Both players stand at one end of a swimming pool with a chessboard on the edge. The first player makes their opening move then sets off down the pool. When they are exactly at the other end, their opponent makes a move and sets off swimming too. By now the first player has returned to the board and has to make his second move – quickly – because players win either by catching up with the other player in the pool, or by actually winning the chess match.

A game both physically and mentally exhausting, it is important that both players should be evenly matched swimmers to make the game as interesting as possible.

Chess Boxing, a very odd combined sport, was invented in a graphic novel by artist Enki Bilal. It was first played in real life in 2003 after being taken up by another artist, Iepe Rubingh.

Chess Boxing, possibly the ultimate combination of physical and mental sports and possibly the stupidest game ever invented, consists of eleven alternate rounds of chess and boxing. The six chess rounds are each four minutes long, so each competitor is only allowed a total of twelve minutes to make all of their moves. The alternating boxing rounds are two minutes long. Victory is by checkmate, a knockout or a judge's decision.

The game's main weakness is that if one of the players is a much superior boxer than the other, the contest will be over almost as soon as the first boxing round starts. Perhaps because of this the game seems to have been quite slow to take off, which is a shame because Britain's Chris Eubank would almost certainly be a good bet for world champion.

Reports that a combined game called Tiddly Wink Kick Boxing has been created in Finland are currently unconfirmed.

Badfight/Badminton Fighting

Badminton Fighting, or Badfight, is another unusual combination sport. Created by Michael Semenenko from St Petersburg State University, it combines badminton and the sort of arm and leg movements you might make in a martial art.

Badfight is played on a 6m by 12m area with a badminton net set at 2m high in the centre. Players tape flat sponge pads, measuring approximately 15cm square, onto the backs of both hands and also onto the tops of their feet. The serving player must kick a shuttlecock over the net. The returning player has two moves to return it; first with the foot and then with the hand. To catch and flick up a shuttlecock using just your foot pad and then to smash it back over the net with the hand pad takes a lot of agility, and the game is exhausting to play.

If the shuttle touches the floor or goes out of bounds, the point is lost. The first player to win fifteen points, wins.

Bat and Trap/Stick Baseball

Bat and Trap is an ancient ball game; a precursor to cricket that also seems to contain elements of baseball, bowls, and even rugby. It is like cricket, except the batting player doesn't run and the fielding team bowls after the batter has batted.

Two teams of eight compete on a narrow pitch that is 21m long by 14m wide. The batting player stands by a see-saw-type lever on the ground that, once they hit it with their bat, throws a ball into the air. The player now has three attempts with this method to try to send this ball between two vertical poles at the end of the pitch. If they do so they score, as long as the fielding players who stand beyond the poles don't catch them out. Now the fielding side bowls at the player.

On the front of the ball-launching device is a small square target which one of the fielders attempts to hit and knock over to get the player out.

Kent contains most of the country's Bat and Trappers, with Canterbury being the main centre for the game.

Bat and Trap is possibly the inspiration for the American street game of **Stick Baseball**. Here the baseball is replaced with a short stick, which at the start of the game is laid resting across a larger stick on the ground. The batting player then uses his bat to hit down on the small stick, causing it to flip into the air where it can be struck with the bat. The game is played thereafter as regular baseball – except with the stick replacing the ball.

Irish Road Bowling

Irish Road Bowling has been played on the country roads of Northern Ireland for over two hundred years (being particularly common in County Armagh), and in recent years has started to grow in popularity in America and Holland.

The game, a sort of marbles for grown ups, consists of teams bowling a tennis-ball-sized iron ball along a set course of country roads; the aim being to complete the course in as few rolls as possible. If the ball comes off the road, into a ditch or field, it is brought back to the nearest bit of road and rolled from there. Any sharp bends in the road are navigated by means of throwing the ball through the air.

Irish Road Bowling is a team game, with non-bowlers helping to determine optimum bowl directions and with one player standing ahead, legs apart, the gap indicating the perfect line. Events are held over different lengths of roads, but a good result for 3.5km would be to finish it in thirty rolls, an average of over 100m per roll.

Krispy Kreme Challenge

If you are trying to lose weight moderate exercise is a great way to shed a few excess pounds, but attempting the **Krispy Kreme Challenge** should probably be avoided. The perfect sporting event for all budding Homer Simpsons is held annually in Raleigh, North Carolina. The challenge is a calorific charity event that was devised by students at the State University in 2004.

Competitors run downhill the two miles to the nearest Krispy Kreme bakery where they have to eat a dozen doughnuts then run the two miles back to the starting line, all within the space of an hour and all the while keeping the doughnuts down. A set of vomit bins greet the struggling competitors who make it to the finishing line.

The average person burns 600 calories on a four-mile jog; unfortunately a dozen doughnuts contain 2,400 calories and over twice the daily recommended allowance of sugar.

From modest beginnings the race now attracts upwards of 3,000 runners and 36,000 doughnuts.

Crap Surfing

If you've ever enjoyed some activity or other but struggled valiantly to become competent at it, your heart will be warmed by **Crap Surfing**. Being rubbish at surfing is probably a world-wide phenomena, but it finds its peak in the UK and is officially recognised in Cornwall where the Crap Surfing World Championships are held in December.

The idea behind the group is genuine, in that it is for people who want to get better at the sport without worrying about being uncool. The group wants to attract surfers who are atypical to the usual surfing stereotypes, or just plain ashamed of not being very good. Members can share their incompetencies and admit how bad they are without guilt or humiliation. If you get exceptionally tired after just paddling out to the waves, or trip over your leash when you get out of the water, or even if you live nowhere near the sea – this is the surf club for you.

As the crap surfing website so succinctly puts it:

'If you have any worries about being: fat, old, unfit, uncoordinated, uncool, intelligent, having the wrong sunglasses, having open-toed sandals with light brown socks, etc., fear not, for you will fit in perfectly because all are welcome and everyone laughs at everyone else'.

Dyke Jumping

Dyke Jumping, or *Fierljeppen*, is probably the only sport that has been developed from a criminal activity. It began in Holland, allegedly, as a means for egg poachers to get over canals surrounding farmers' fields and then escape again before getting caught. Today it is a fully regulated game with national championships and teams of jumpers in Belgium and even Japan.

Dyke Jumping is a combination of pole vaulting and rope climbing and is a highly skilled activity. The jumpers take off from jetties that are 2m above the water level and run towards a 10m pole which is resting against this jetty. Skilled jumpers will hit the pole at exactly the right speed so that it will slowly reach its most upright position, giving them as much time as possible to scramble up it before it starts its descent to the other bank. (The time a competitor stays on the pole is, impressively, around the 4-second mark.) As the pole approaches the far side of the canal the jumper has to pick the optimum time to leap off it. The person jumping the furthest, wins.

The canal used is 12m wide with sand beyond that. The current world record is 19.5m.

Greased Games

Greased Pole Climbing is not just a metaphor for life's struggles but is actually played as a game at festivals in Thailand, Taiwan and Sri Lanka.

Generally, it is a team game with members making group attempts to get to the top of a 12m, greased wooden pole. The aim is usually to get to the top to collect a flag placed there, although sometimes bank notes are attached to the pole at various heights to spur on competitors.

The successful climbing method is a combination of sand on the hands, balancing on teammates' shoulders and taking it in turns to climb ever higher sections of the pole whilst trying to wipe off the grease above you with rags. At some events it can take a team many hours and a lot of cramped thighs before the pole is conquered.

A great Inuit game that deserves wider attention is **Greased Pole Walking**. Fix a log the size of a telephone pole horizontally on the ground and cover it liberally with grease (use seal fat if you want to be authentic, but cooking lard makes an acceptable alternative). Now players take it in turns to see who can walk barefoot the furthest along the pole without falling off. Apparently this game develops all the necessary skills needed to creep up close to prey in icy conditions.

Greased Pig Wrestling is the preserve of the American county fair. This is a team event where four players attempt to grab hold of a greased pig in a pen – or at least a pig that has been covered in slippery wet mud – and then try to wrestle it into a barrel. The origin of this bizarre and cruel activity is unknown. Sometimes a children's version of the event is held, the Greased Pig Contest, where kids just have to hold on to a greased pig, or piglet, for a set amount of time.

Hanetball

Hanetball is the game you would get if you crossed a game of basketball with a trip to a baby supplies store. The game is currently played in Florida but expect, as its creator calls it, 'THE game of the twentieth century' to make an appearance near you soon.

The game is played with two teams of seven players using a Hanetball (basically a basketball) on a rectangular court (similar to the one used in basketball) and the ball must be bounced when running with it (a little like basketball) but – and it's a big but – instead of being fixed to the walls the baskets are souped-up toddler playpens. Large (3.5m diameter) circular playpens with netted sides are placed at both ends of the court and inside them stands the team's goalkeeper, who tries to repel any ball that the opponents attempt to throw into the net. Games comprise of four quarters and last seventy minutes, or until the goalkeeper cries to be let out.

Strange Running

The downhill running of fell runners is a little peculiar, but if you want to take part in some really strange running you should consider **Slalom Running**. Like the winter sport of Giant Slalom Ski-ing, you need some flags and as steep a slope as possible, but not the snow. Slalom Running made an appearance in 2002 on the Channel Five show *International King of Sports*, a sports parody show where real athletes competed in a combination of made-up games and silly things that you used to play as a kid. To play, simply set up gates made from the flags (jumpers will do) at intervals down the slope. Players now take it in turns to slalom-run down the slope, between all the gates, in the fastest time possible.

Slalom Running was set to play a part in the 2000 Fringe Games in Christchurch, New Zealand. These games, which were planned but never got to fruition, were to be an alternative to the Sydney Olympics. The Slalom Running differed in that it was done on the flat along with a whole host of unusual athletic events such as backwards and sideways running, assisted jumping, etc. The highlight though would have been the **Formation Running** event. Formation Running is for teams of four players; each wears a belt and is attached to their neighbouring runner by a short piece of bungee-type rope. Linked together in a row like this, the team now runs around the track in a line behind the leader, competing against other teams joined up in the same way. For the sport to work, teammates should be of equivalent athletic ability, as lagging behind can have serious consequences for yourself and the rest of the team.

Backwards Running or, as it is more usually called, **Retro Running** came to prominence as an organised sport in the 1980s in the US and Europe. Perhaps unsurprisingly, one of the European countries most keen on the retreating sport of running backwards is Italy, where the annual Golden Shrimp race is one of the sport's most prestigious. Retro Running has the advantage of working a totally different set of muscles to forwards running and burns up to a third more calories. It has the major disadvantage of making people laugh at you when you are out training.

World record times for the 200m is 32 seconds, and for the Backwards Marathon (or should that be Nohtaram) 3 hours, 43 minutes.

High-heel Racing

High-heel Racing, or Stiletto Running, is exactly as it says on the tin: running as fast as possible whilst wearing stiletto-heeled shoes. In the last few years the sport has taken off in Europe, with large organised events taking place in Russia, Germany, Holland and Poland.

The minimal rules state that the shoes worn must have a heel of 7cm or longer, with a tip of a diameter of no more than 1.5cm (which means you will be dis-qualified if you turn up in your 1970s platform heels). At 2007's Berlin race, competitor Denise Hanitsch won the 100m race in a stunning time of 14.7 seconds. But Europe cannot claim High-heel Racing as its own; there is an annual High-heel Race held by local drag queens in Washington DC which is now into its twentieth year.

It must be time for the idea behind this marvellous sport to be extended to other track events. The High-heel Hurdles would surely be an event worth staging.

Mud Glorious Mud

Maldon, in Essex, hosts the world's greatest Mud Run, known locally as the **Mad Maldon Mud Run**. It happens annually in late December/early January when there is a very low tide. Competitors, which number almost two hundred, attempt to run across the River Blackwater, along its far bank and back across the river again. The total distance run is only about 600m, but the whole course is either waist-deep water or knee- to thigh-length viciously smelling mud. Most competitors, many in fancy dress, stumble and crawl through the mud before being hosed down at the end. Rules are few, except that no swimming is allowed.

Mud Tugging, by comparison, is almost a popular sport and is at its most common in America. The basic concept being a tug-of-war with a mud pit between the two teams, or sometimes actually the whole competition taking place in the mire.

The true kings of mud games, though, may well be the Chinese. The sporting event called, enlighteningly, '**Crazy for Mud**' kicks off a whole Sea Mud Carnival on a Xiushan Island beach in China's Zhejiang Pronvince. Mud games including racing, Mud Skating and, of course, Tug-of-War are all played in thick and deep sea mud. However, the highlight comes in the form of competitive Mud Wife Carrying – a short sprint through knee-deep mud carrying your 'wife'. A brilliant combination game. How come the Finns haven't thought of that?

Mob Football

Mob Football is a sport that began in medieval times and was the ugly precursor to the beautiful game of modern football. All around Europe during this time similar games, usually played on festival days, sprang up that involved the whole male population of adjoining villages trying to drag a ball from one village to the next using any means possible. Games were long and violent to the point of causing some players' deaths. The games suffered attempted bans by a succession of kings and church leaders, but thankfully some versions have survived to the present day.

The Ba' is a mob game that is played on Christmas Day and New Year's Day in Kirkwall, Orkney Isles, Scotland. The two teams both come from the town, but depending on where they were born relative to the cathedral they are called either 'Uppies' or 'Doonies'.

Hundreds of players play on each side and once the game has kicked off massive scrums form as the Uppies try to force the 1.3kg ball southwards and the Doonies northwards. Games have lasted five hours or more, with tactics including pretending to have the ball and making a distracting run down narrow lanes in the town, to even taking the game up to rooftop level.

A similar game, **The Jedburgh Hand Ba' Game**, is played in the border town of Jedburgh on Shrove Tuesday. Dating from the seventeenth century, it is alleged to have been first played with the severed heads of English invaders.

The Haxey Hood game is played annually in Haxey, Lincolnshire, on Twelfth Day. The game began in the fourteenth century when Lady de Mowbray's riding hood was blown from her head into a field of farm workers.

Today, the game begins after an elaborate set of traditional events and processions, tours of pubs, metaphorical shenanigans with staffs and setting fire to the village fool.

The Hood, which is a long leather tube, is released into the throng – a couple of hundred players called the 'Sway'. Their aim is to move the hood to one of four local pubs, where the game will end as soon as the pub's landlord has touched the hood. The hood cannot be thrown and it can't even be run with but must be swayed along by teams not readily distinguishable from one other.

Predictably, games last many hours and everything in the path of the Sway is at risk of damage.

Possibly the most famous mob football game is **The Royal Ashbourne Shrovetide Football Game**. This has been played for many hundreds of years and takes place in Ashbourne, Derbyshire, on two days: Shrove Tuesday and Ash Wednesday.

Like The Ba', the two teams are defined by their geographical location. The Up'ards were born north of the River Henmore and the Down'ards south. Crowds of up to 5,000 watch as the hand-painted ball is dropped into the scrum (known as the Hug) of hundreds of players. The spectators see very little of the ball from that point as it is held within the Sway. The goals are set three miles apart and one team wins if they can tap the ball three times against the goal board. The most basic of rules are: to keep off church property, no hiding of the ball in bags and no transporting of the ball in cars. An old rule used to be: no murdering!

Any player that scores a goal gets to keep it as a trophy.

In 2003 Prince Charles set off proceedings by dropping the ball into the Sway, but unfortunately he didn't get involved in the game itself.

Mosquito Squashing

There is a rather juvenile summer garden game where you wait for a mosquito to land on someone, preferably on some sensitive spot like their neck or bare legs, then you slap it hard – killing the mosquito and giving the person a stinging blow while all the time watching your own back for the person trying to squash one on you.

It has taken the Finns to run with this idea and make it into a summer festival. **The World Mosquito Killing Championships** began in 1993 and has occurred annually ever since. The event, which takes place in Pelkosenniemi, Northern Finland, in July, is based around squashing as many mosquitoes as possible in five minutes. The main rule is that they must be dispatched by hand; no machines or chemicals are allowed. The World Record, held by Finn Henri Pellonpää, is twenty-one in five minutes.

In the last two years, however, the event has not taken place because dry weather has meant there have been insufficient mosquitoes. Is Mosquito Squashing going to

be the first strange game to be stopped due to global warming? Will Arse-Leather Sledging follow and fade away before it even has a chance to establish itself?

Pedal Car Racing

When you think of pedal cars you probably remember the vehicle you had as a toddler which moved slowly and erratically until you got it going downhill, whereupon you were pedaling so quickly and out of control that you'd smash your knees to pieces against the inside of the frame.

Pedal Car Racing, as run in the British Pedal Car Championships, is a much more serious affair.

The cars raced are hand-built creations and totally human powered – using bicycle pedals and gearing systems. The cars are designed on the outside to be very stylish, almost like 1950s Formula 1 cars – all sleek, bullet-shaped bodies but sitting on what look like large, old-fashioned pram wheels instead.

Each car weighs around 25kg and travels at a respectable 25 miles per hour. Just like Formula 1, there are back-up teams for each car (engineers, spare drivers, timers) and pit stops. The British Championships are decided on with an eight-leg series at different venues around the country. These races vary in length from 100-mile events to a gruelling Le Mans-style 24-hour race in Swansea.

Strange Games with Sheep

Any game that involves children, animals being dressed up and wrestling, and which incurs the wrath of animal rights groups has surely got to be worthy of investigation. **Sheep Tackling**, or to give it its Latin name Ovis Overpowering, is one such game.

Simply get five sheep and dress them up in rugby shirts. Then get the players (in this case five hundred primary-school children) to chase the sheep around a rugby pitch trying to wrestle them to the ground. The first group of players to successfully ground and immobilise a sheep are the winners.

Sheep Tackling is apparently a traditional method of honing rugby skills for players in rural New Zealand and it is a popular half-time entertainment at some rugby matches in some parts of the country. The sheep wear the team's rugby shirts which, being a little on the big side, hamper the sheep's movement. Even so, they still outrun the children for most of the time. Sheep Tackling is now rightly banned, following criticism from The Society for the Prevention of Cruelty to Animals.

Another woolly Antipodean game is **The Sheep Counting World Championships** which happen in Hay, Australia. The competition is simple: hundreds of sheep run past the players and all they have to do is count how many there are as accurately as possible. The world record is a correct count of 277.

Watermelon Ski-ing

The first recorded watermelon harvest occurred nearly 5,000 years ago in Egypt and is depicted in Egyptian hieroglyphics on walls of their ancient buildings. Watermelons were often placed in the burial tombs of their kings to nourish them in the afterlife. It took the Australians to strap them to their feet and make a sport out of it.

Every two years, the town of Chinchilla, in Queensland, pays tribute to the melon harvest with the **Chinchilla Melon Festival**, where people not only eat the melons but use them for a number of other activities, such as melon bungee, pip spitting, and even head-butting them. The highlight of the festival, however, is **Watermelon Ski-ing**.

For this event players put down a long tarpaulin and make it as slippery as possible – the insides of a few dozen watermelons make a grand lubricant. Then players take it in turns to stand at the beginning of the run, each foot encased in a scooped-out watermelon. They hold on to a rope being held by two people standing either side of the tarpaulin, who then run down the course dragging the watermelon skier behind them. The person who remains on their feet and in their watermelon shoes for the longest distance is the winner.

In Britain local councils are nervous of having Bunny Hopping Races in case people fall over and sue, while the good people of Chinchilla are strapping melons onto their feet and dragging each other into oblivion.

For more watermelon fun you can always try **Greased Watermelon Polo**. Simply cover a larger watermelon with vaseline, or other lubricant, and throw it into the middle of a swimming pool. Watermelons float. Two teams of players now jump into the pool and have to get the slippery fruit to their own end using any means possible.

Wife Carrying

In the 1800s in Finland it was common to farm moose, drink heavily and steal women from neighbouring villages, yet only one of these activities became a competitive sport. **The Wife Carrying World Championships** occur annually in Sankajarvi, Finland.

The carry is over a 253m course made up of obstacles that include hurdles, slopes and a 1m-deep water section (the Restricted-height Wife Carrying Championships never really got off the ground). The 'wife' does not HAVE to be the competitor's own, but she must weigh at least 49kg. Lighter models have weights added to them to even up the competition and to put a stop to all those size-zero entrants. The method of carrying is entirely up to competitors, but the most successful appears to be what is known as the 'Estonian Carry', with the wife upside down on the carrier's back, her arms around his waist and her legs over his shoulders. Time penalties of 15 seconds are added if you drop your wife and the fastest couple over the course wins the prize of the wife's weight in beer. The current world record for the course is 1 minute 1 second.

Two further events at the same Championships are the Wife Carrying Triathlon and Wife Relay. The relay has three men carrying one wife over the course and the Triathlon involves walking sideways and over the main course with water features whilst carrying, and then cycling with the wife balanced on the bike.

The nearest equivalent to Wife Carrying in the UK is probably the **Ponteland Wheelbarrow Races**. On New Year's Day, competitors race as a pair over a mile-long

course in the village of Ponteland, with one in a wheelbarrow and one pushing. The record time is an impressive 8 minutes.

Pewsey Wheelbeero Race

Pewsey, a village in Wiltshire, holds a town festival in September each year. The usual processions and carnival queens are present and correct, but the village does appear to have a liking for what can only be described as drink-driving events. The key event is the aptly titled **Pewsey Wheelbeero Race**.

Teams are formed of three people and a wheelbarrow. One sits in the barrow whilst the other two push them around a two-mile course, which in one part goes through the river around the village centre. Teams are themed and dressed like any other parade, but the main rule states that each member should drink at least one pint of beer in each hostelry along the course.

If you want more sophistication in your rat-arsed racing you should enter the **Pewsey Wine Race**. This has similar principles to the Wheelbeero, except here a team of four are bound together at the ankles and must complete the same course but drink a glass of wine in each pub.

And the kids haven't been left out: they have the **Kids Sedan Race**. Three kids must enter per team; one is carried in a sedan chair by the other two and they all drink a soft drink in each pub.

One can't help but think that Pewsey are missing a trick by not holding the ASBO Carry – two teenagers in hoodies carry a third around the course while sinking a bottle of cheap cider in each establishment.

Woolsack Racing

Although lacking the unusual carry of Finnish Wife Carrying or the weight and distance of Coal Carrying, **Woolsack Racing** is still a British carrying game to cherish. Woolsack Racing is held at the end of the May Bank Holiday in Tetbury, Gloucestershire. The town, which was a major wool producer in the sixteenth century, has been having a Woolsack Day for centuries.

Competitors must run a course of 240m up Gumstool Hill (which in places has a gradient of 1 in 4) whilst carrying a 27kg sack of wool on their shoulders. There are both relay and individual events, a women's race (where the sacks are a mere 16kg) and even a youth race.

The winner of the 2006 race finished the course in a respectable 48 seconds.

World Coal Carrying Championships

Coal Carrying is a competitive sport which, like Nettle Eating, began as an argument in a pub between two men. In this case it was in 1963 in a pub in Gawthorpe, near Wakefield, Yorkshire, and the argument between a coal merchant and his friend about who was the fittest led to the creation of the World Coal Carrying Championships.

The race has been run ever since on Easter Monday and involves racing whilst carrying a 50kg bag of coal over a course of 0.7 of a mile. The race starts off at the Royal Oak Pub and finishes at the maypole on the village green. There is a women's race in which they used to carry only 11kg but now carry the same weight of coal as the men and even children's categories.

The world record time is 4 minutes 6 seconds.

A more recent addition to the world of coal carrying is the **Scottish Coal Carrying Championship** which takes place in Kelty. The race is run over a course of a similar length (1,000m) with men carrying 50kg and ladies 25kg.

World Crazy Golf Championships

If you have ever enjoyed a windswept August afternoon on a concrete and fake-grass golf course as seagulls dive bomb you just as you are trying to get the ball past the sails of a windmill and through the Arc de Triomphe – then **Minigolf** may be the game for you.

Re-branded from Crazy Golf (possibly because of negative connotations with sports for the mentally ill), Minigolf is basically the same game that is played at coastal resorts around the country. It now has its own governing body – the World Minigolf Sport Federation – and a set of championships throughout the year. Minigolf events are held everywhere from the Southend Masters to the World Championships (which in 2007 was in Italy), and the prize money on offer is surprising: £1000 for winning the British Open.

A championship-level course should be designed with 18 holes to test a player's putting skills, his ability to calculate angles off curved barriers and, most importantly, his sense of humour.

The record round is a stunning 18 – a hole in one at every hole, even the one where you have to go over the little see-saw.

The world of **Office Golf** is starting to become more structured now, with sponsored events taking place in New York and London. A set of holes are placed around offices, sometimes on different floors, leading to that tricky-to-time lift shot, and with ready-made obstacles from chairs to filing cabinets brought into play. Whisky-makers Glenlivet have organised regular events with hundreds of companies taking part.

The Ice Golf World Championships is a unique event that is played annually in March in Uummannaq, Greenland. The 9-hole course is created on sea ice with the natural ice features forming hazards and specially smoothed 'greens'. Due to global warming the event has had to be cancelled in 2004, 2005 and 2007 because of dangerously thin ice.

World Pooh Sticks Championships

Although the game of **Pooh Sticks** was created by A A Milne in 1926, it took until 1983 for a World Championship to be established, and this happened partly by chance. A local lock-keeper in Oxfordshire noticed that people often played Pooh sticks there, so he started the Championships as a charity fundraiser.

They have been held ever since at Day's Lock, Little Wittenham, with entrants being both local and international; players have come from Latvia and Pakistan, and Japan took the team event title one year.

The bridge that apparently inspired A A Milne to create the game is actually 66 miles away in Ashdown Forest, Sussex.

The Eight Rules of Pooh Sticks (with apologies to *Fight Club*):

Rule 1: You do not talk about Pooh Sticks.
Rule 2: You DO NOT talk about Pooh Sticks.
Rule 3: When someone says 'Drop!' you must release your stick; NEVER throw your stick.
Rule 4: Only one game of Pooh Sticks at a time.
Rule 5: Sticks used must be found in the area around the bridge.
Rule 6: Players cannot pull off parts of the bridge to use as sticks.
Rule 7: The first stick to appear on the other side of the bridge is the winner.
Rule 8: If this is your first time at Pooh Sticks, you MUST play.

World Sauna Championships

It appears the Finns can make a weird sport or World Championship out of anything.

The World Sauna Championships take place in Heinola, Finland, every year in August.

The saunas, which have large steam-free windows so that spectators can easily see in, are kept at a constant temperature of 110 degrees Celsius (a normal sauna is kept at 80 degrees Celsius) and during the competition water is thrown on the heater every 30 seconds. All you have to do is stay in as long as possible.

Competitors, who wear swimming costumes, must sit with their thighs touching the wooden benches and in an upright position. No sprawling or trying to psyche out the other competitors is allowed. Presumably that means that you can't strike up idle conversation like, 'Warm, for the time of year', or start humming Nelly's *It's Getting Hot in Here*.

One further rule is that to have their time count competitors must leave the sauna under their own steam, so to speak. Referees are on hand to make sure no-one is badly burnt and to extract players who look like they've had enough. Players enter from all around the world but especially the Baltic States and, of course, a Finn wins. Many can't get past the 5- or 6-minute mark, but the world record stands at a sweltering 16 minutes.

STAND-OFF GAMES

Stand-off games, usually for two players only, are those where you must each perform the same activity but do it to your opponent and do it before he does it to you. For example, footstamping or the Cotswold Olimpick Sport of Shin Kicking.

The Stanga Games

The Stanga Games, or the Gotlandic Olympics, is a three-day event that has taken place in Gotland, Sweden, since 1924 and includes an array of unusual games – many of them classic stand-off games. It's a sort of Swedish version of the Scottish Highland Games.

The **Kick Astride** game (known as Spark Blaistre in Sweden, or kicking the strip) is a great stand-off game that uses a rope. Each player ties one end of a 20m rope tightly around his ankle. They both begin by standing closer than 20m apart and then the aim of the game is to get their opponent to fall over first. This is achieved by kicking their leg in order to make the rope do the work of pulling over the other player. As in all classic stand offs, players have to take the decision about how hard to attack the opponent, as often trying too hard can prove your own downfall.

Pillow Fighting over a muddy pit, or *Varst Kallingg Pa Stangg* (best lady on the bar), is as simple as its English title: a log is suspended over a muddy pit. Two players sit astride the log with pillows in hand; both hands must remain off the pole at all times and the first to land in the mud loses.

In America, Pillow Fighting has a world championship which occurs annually in Kenwood, California, on 4 July.

Breaking The Ox involves more rope and mud, but this time the two players have a large loop of rope which they place over their chests and face away from each other. Between them is a pool of mud. They must pull using chest and leg power to force the other into the mud.

Native American Stand-off Games

In Native-American culture many of the games are stand-off in nature; arm, leg and thumb wrestling are all old Native-American games. As are:

Tug of Pole, in which players sit down opposite each other with the soles of their feet touching. Each holds onto the same stick with both hands fairly spaced. Now the aim is to bring the other person to a standing position just by pulling on the stick. No other body movement is allowed and feet should remain firmly fixed together.

Staff Wrestling again uses a stick but players lay down on the ground facing each other, head to head and on their stomachs. Their outstretched arms both hold onto the same short stick. Hands must be arranged alternately and evenly so that each of the players has one of their hands at a stick end. The aim is to flip your opponent onto their back before they flip you onto yours, which takes great control and upper-arm strength.

Inuit Stand-off Games

Inuit culture has a number of excellent stand-off games such as Back to Back Pushing, Ear Pulling (a more painful version of Goanna Pulling (see page 208), where the straps are attached to the ears rather than the neck).

For **Finger Pulling,** players sit on the floor facing their opponent then place their feet against each other. Players now link index fingers by making them into a hook shape, and pull against each other using their feet as leverage. The first player to straighten their finger, loses.

A similar game is played in Pflugdorf, Munich. **German Finger Wrestling** (*Fingerhakeln*) is played annually as part of the Bavarian Pentathlon (the other sports being log sawing, stein lifting, boulder lifting and dumpling eating). Here, players attach a small leather loop to their index finger and face each other from opposite sides of a table, the aim being to drag their opponent over to their side using finger power alone.

Mouth Pulling is a truly odd stand-off game which you won't want to play if you have issues with hygiene and pain. For two players at a time; stand closely side by side and place your adjacent arms over one another's shoulders, then place your index finger inside your neighbour's mouth and hook it into the side of their cheek. They do the same to you. Now start pulling. The first to give in, loses. No biting is allowed.

The native Inuit game of **Ear Pulling** is occasionally played as a game in the Arctic Winter Games, although even here they often try to forget about it due to the frequent injuries/possible injuries that can be caused by it.

In this classic stand-off game the two contestants face each other across a line drawn on the floor and both have a thin connecting loop of leather placed

around their left ears. Now, simply, they pull backwards with their heads and have an aural tug-of-war – the aim being to pull the other over the central line or give up in pain.

Nose Licking

A really odd stand-off game, what **Nose Licking** lacks in hygiene it makes up for in fun and stupidity.

For two players; each faces the other and holds the other's shoulders. This hold must be maintained throughout the game. Now each player attempts to lick the nose of their opponent whilst all the time trying to avoid having their own nose licked. Games tend to have an initial phase where both players maintain their distance, but generally they soon come to realise that if they are going to grasp victory they are going to have to get closer and lick that nose.

Battle Lautrec

A bizarre, imbecilic game for two people, **Battle Lautrec** is guaranteed to banish boredom and raise a smile at the very least.

To play you must first master the Lautrec balance – named after the French artist of restricted height. To do this you kneel on the floor then reach behind your knees, grab an ankle in each hand and lift up your lower legs. With practice you should then be able to balance and move around, albeit quite slowly at first, on your knees. You must keep hold of your ankles at all times.

Now the battle: face your opponent, go into a Lautrec balance and try to make them lose their balance and fall. You may use any means open to you – body weight or pushing with your head or shoulders. The first person to release hold of their ankles or fall flat on their face is the loser.

For even more fun, start the battle at opposite ends of the room so that you have to knee-walk a reasonable distance before battle commences. Long-term players may want to improvise some sort of knee pad to reduce wear and tear on their knees.

For extreme fun, try playing with a scattering of marbles on the floor.

Knee Balance Burn

You can't beat a party game with a lit candle for the wonderful feeling that you may be sued at any moment by a litigious parent. And all because little Jimmy suffered minor burns... **Knee Balance Burn** is one such game.

For two players at a time. Each faces the other, then both players go into a single knee balance – a great skill to learn and one that is bound to come in useful in later life. One player holds a lighted candle in one hand only, the other player holds an unlighted one. Their aim is to touch candles and get the unlighted candle lit before their raised knees touch the floor. If they fail, it is someone else's turn. The team that performs the task fastest and without burns, wins.

Hat Dance and Motorcycle Ninja

Hat Dance is a fun stand-off party game. It's easy to play and always has everyone howling with laughter, especially the onlookers. Two people wear party hats. Each tries to knock off the other person's hat first. (Lots of leaning back and slapping action.) For an interesting variation, get each player to wear a motorbike crash helmet with an elastic-stringed party hat on top. Furnish both players with a toy plastic sword and you have – **Motorcycle Ninja**.

Ankle Battle

To be successful at **Ankle Battle** you will need strong muscles and the balance of a cat.

Each player faces the other then lifts their left leg and holds it at the ankle with their left hand. Balancing like this on one foot, each player must now hold his opponent's right hand in a firm grasp and, without losing their grip or releasing their left ankle, they must try to pull the other player over.

The first player to either release their left ankle or fall in an undignified heap onto the floor is the loser. For terrifyingly good fun, try playing the game blindfolded.

Two Dogs and a Bone

Two Dogs and a Bone is a great, dynamic stand-off game.

A stick or baton (the 'bone') is placed in the centre of the room. The players are split into two groups and each individual is allocated a number to remember. So, if there are ten players there will be numbers one to five on each team. The teams line up opposite their opposing numbers at either end of the room and equidistant from the baton. A caller shouts out a number of their choosing; those two players must rush to try to get the baton first and return it to their team to win. However, if they are tagged when they are carrying it the opposing team wins.

The most important rule is that no player can cross (with their feet) the centre line of the room on which the baton stands before it is grabbed. Once one has it, the other player can enter the other half of the hall to try and tag. This rule leads to tense and thrilling stand–offs, with both players hovering around the baton waiting for the other to grab first, followed by a mad chase back.

Marker Pen Fighting

Marker Pen Fighting is a silly stand-off-type game from the playground that usually ends in tears; at least, it should if it's played properly.

For two or more players, each is armed with a non-permanent, large, felt-tipped marker pen (the type that are used on white boards). Each player must now try to cover their opponents with marker-pen ink, both on clothes and skin, whilst trying to avoid being marked much themselves. In practice this usually ends up as a wild free-for-all leading to much sorrow and scrubbing of skin.

Goanna Pulling

The Australians are never a nation to do things by half measures, and so it is with their stand-off game inspired by lizards. **Goanna Pulling** is the only game in the world that combines feats of massive strength with reptile impersonations.

Apparently dating from the nineteenth century, the Goanna Pulling Competition takes place in Wooli, Australia. Contestants lie on their stomachs facing each other and with their hands they raise their upper body off the ground, thus making their bodies a bit lizard-like. They are attached to one another by a short leather strap with loops on the end which go around the neck of each player. By scuttling backwards (in the style of an goanna, hence the name) they then try to pull the others over a central line using mainly neck and arm strength. They should retain the lizard stance throughout the contest.

Trussed Fowls

A truly bizarre game, **Trussed Fowls** is for two players at a time. Each is trussed – which means that both their ankles and wrists must be bound – then each crouches down with their arms over their knees and a broom handle is threaded over their elbows and under both knees. The player is now trussed like a chicken and will have very limited movement.

Both players are now placed head to head. Their aim is to knock over their opponent using any means left to them – which are obviously few and far between. What follows is lots of chicken-like hopping and helpless falling over.

Trussed Fowls used to be a really popular game around 1900 and took on various names, including Cock Fighting. Even with the more acceptable name of Trussed Fowls it's hard to see its revival occurring at today's children's parties. Of course, one can but hope.

The Clapping Game/Belly Button Bounce-off

If you want to play a game that needs a combination of balance, timing and power, and one that illustrates Newton's third law, **The Clapping Game** is the one for you.

For two players: stand as close together as possible, facing each other with toes touching, so you are almost but not quite falling backwards. Then, on a count of three, each player raises both hands and tries to push their opponent backwards by pushing against their hands only. What usually happens is that players frantically clap against the other's hands trying to get them to unbalance but not wanting

to push too hard in case they fall over themselves.
If both players remain in position, continue until a winner is found.

There is a stomach-based variation of the game called **Belly Button Bounce-off**. Two players stand facing each other, as close as possible, feet together, their stomachs touching. On an agreed signal both players start to push the other using their stomachs only; a solid stomach along with a Beyoncé-like thrust of the hips make for a winning combination. The first player to take a step backwards is the loser.

Games involving racing animals of the same species have been popular ever since Lassie challenged Digby the Biggest Dog in the World to a race after a drunken argument in a Hollywood bar. As well as racing games, also included here are Squirrel Fishing, Beetle Fighting and the brilliant American game of Cow Patty Bingo.

Animal Racing and Jumping

There are scores of strange races involving animals that are held around the world; from small events at village fêtes and county fairs to full-blown world championships. These are some of the most unusual ones, in evolutionary tree order.

Maggot Racing occurs in many places but a well-organised annual race is held in the George and Dragon Pub, Wray village, Lancashire, in March. Maggot Racing is usually run across a 90cm board with strong lights on the starting line that send the maggots crawling on their way.

Slug Racing is the shell-less version of snail racing; it is popular in the US at school fairs. Like snail racing, Slug Racing is usually carried out by putting all the slugs in the centre of a large cardboard disc. First slug to get to the edge, wins.

Goldfish Racing is a very bizarre practice. Each goldfish has its own water-filled perspex lane. Competitors pick their fish then use straws to blow air bubbles into the water behind the fish to encourage them onwards. The winning fish get all excited by their victory then forget all about it.

Cockroach Racing features another animal that is raced in locations around the world, but the Australians have held the World Championships at the Story Bridge Hotel, Brisbane, every January since 1982. The races include straightforward sprints and more challenging steeplechases.

Cockroach Racing is also an event at the Purdue Bug Bowl – home of Cricket Spitting (see page 157).

Frog Jumping features as part of the Frog Jubilee at the Calaveras County Fair, US. The frog that jumps the greatest distance in a single leap, wins, with the world record held by a frog named Rosie the Ribeter who jumped 6.5m.

The World Championships of **Lizard Racing** are held in Eulo, Queensland. Eulo is a one-pub town and was the site for the world's first intersport animal head-to head race between a lizard and a cockroach. Unfortunately the cockroach met an accidental death, spoiling his glory after he had won the competition.

The **Hen Racing** World Championships are held in the Barley Mow Pub, Hensall, Derbyshire. Competitors from around the world add to the ranks of locals vying for the coveted title. Hens have three minutes to reach the finishing line, and if no hen gets there it is the nearest hen that wins.

Ostrich Racing is held at the Annual Ostrich Festival, Chandler, US. Ostrich

Racing involves the birds pulling men in mini-chariots around the course. If only they'd used ostriches in Spartacus.

Rabbit Show Jumping is exactly like horse show jumping, except it has no riders. Rabbit Show Jumping began in the 1970s in Scandinavia, where it is still popular with over fifty clubs. Simply, rabbits jump over rabbit-sized fences.

The UK capital for **Sheep Racing** is Hoo Farm in Telford, which holds regular events including a Grand National featuring up to seventeen sheep running over fences. Goat Racing is also featured at the farm.

Beetle Fighting

Beetle Fighting with real live beetles has been a childhood activity in Thailand and other areas of South-east Asia for many years. It is only in recent times that the game has really taken off, especially so in Japan where top beetles can exchange hands for thousands of pounds.

Traditionally in Thailand the beetle used is Xylotrupes Gideon, or the rhinoceros beetle, to give it its common name. These beetles, 5–7.5cm in length, are so named because they have a large horn-like protusion on the top of their heads. Contests are held on a horizontally placed bamboo pole within which a compartment has been hollowed out to contain a female of the species – in this way she is out of sight of the male beetles but can still be detected by smell. Two male beetles are then placed on the bamboo and the fight begins: beetles tightly grip the pole, lock horns and battle for supremacy while trying to throw one another off. The beetle owners encourage their beetles with a small stick, which when twizzled makes a noise that spurs the beetle on, but if a beetle backs away or refuses to fight or is lifted off its feet they are deemed to have lost. The winning beetle becomes highly prized and will be used to breed from.

Fights are held during the beetle's mating season when this behaviour is a naturally occuring activity. None are harmed during the fighting; in fact, in Thailand a species which was once reducing in numbers is now thriving.

Cow Patty Bingo

Even though it has undergone a makeover, the game of bingo in Britain is hardly the most glamorous of activities; rows of players sitting silently on formica chairs wielding large felt-tip markers as a droning caller tries to bring life to the numbers.

In America they have come up with the ultimate bingo – one that relies on a bovine's bowel activity.

Cow Patty Bingo, or **Cow Drop Raffle** as it is sometimes known, has become a popular charity fund-raising event all across America, and now that the government allows gambling if it is aiding non-profit making organisations, it has become a legal activity.

A field is marked off into squares of equal sizes and these mini-plots of land are sold to players for $5 upwards. Once all squares have been sold, the crowd gathers, the cow is released onto the grass and the tension builds. The crowd now will the cow to defecate, or not, depending on where it is. The cow raising her tail, maybe to swat a fly, raises hopes, and then, once the patty has been delivered, a judge will deliberate if by chance it has fallen and landed across two squares. The winning player gets their cut of the entry money while those whose squares surround the winner's receive smaller prizes.

Eyes down for round two!

Flounder Tramping

Flounder Tramping, a fish-catching game with a difference, was begun in Palnackie, Scotland, in the early 1970s as a fundraiser for the RNLI. The event, which is staged in mid-July, attracts hundreds of people who tramp around Palnackie mud flats trying to catch a flounder (the flat fish *Platychthys Flesus* which can grow up to a size of 50cm) using only their feet. Any fish caught are weighed and released, unharmed, back into the wild.

A game that favours the player who is nimble and has large feet.

American Catfish Noodling

The ancient Romany art of Trout Tickling (you gently tickle a trout's underbelly before grabbing your prey) has been taken by some Americans, made infinitely more brash and turned into the competitive event of **Catfish Noodling**.

Noodling is banned in many US states but is still practised in some Southern ones, being especially popular in Oklahoma. The practice of catching a fish using your hands only is probably a useful skill in times of famine, but Catfish Noodling is both cruel and dangerous. The giant catfish, which can get as big as 45kg, tend to live in rivers in underwater burrows and are captured by thrusting your hand in, waiting for the catfish to bite it and hold on. You then have to pull the fish out of its hiding place and wrestle it to the surface to complete the noodle.

Many noodlers suffer severe catfish bites to the hand as well as bites from water snakes, and there is the odd case of drowning.

Man Versus Horse

There was an American television series in 2003, of especially dubious taste, called *Man vs Beast*. In it wild animals would compete against humans in a variety of odd, sometimes disturbing acts. For example, who can eat the most sausages – competitive-eating champion or grizzly bear? And possibly the weirdest show where forty-four 'Little People' competed against an elephant to see who could pull a passenger plane a short distance in the quickest time. The elephant won. The pilot show for the UK version, hosted by John Fashanu, was never shown because of strong objections from animal rights groups.

The Man Versus Horse race has not been created for television, it is instead an odd race that has been run in Wales for over twenty years.

It has the perfect pedigree for a strange game, in that it was the first held because of an argument in a pub and it occurs in Llanwrtyd Wells, home to Bog Snorkelling and Mountain Bike Bog Snorkelling. In the event, men and horses compete in a 22-mile marathon through the Welsh countryside. Over five hundred runners and forty horses compete, and a horse has won every single year except in 2004 when marathon-runner Huw Lobb beat all comers.

Squirrel Fishing

Squirrel Fishing as a game came to prominence in the 1990s in US colleges. It has since spread as a pastime around the country.

The basic idea is that you tie a peanut, or your favourite bait, onto the end of a piece of string and wait for one of the bushy-tailed rodents to take the bait. If you want to play competitively, however, you need some sort of points system. One that has been suggested, by a Harvard study of the game, is that if a squirrel touches your bait you get a point. You get two points if it eats some of the bait and a full three points if you can then drag the squirrel a short distance. The ultimate objective is to be able to lift the squirrel off the ground for any length of time. The game is then won.

The squirrels are never harmed in the game.

It is the sort of activity that maybe Ernest Hemingway would enjoy – if he were alive today and had a sense of humour.

World Snail Racing

Possibly the greatest form of racing involving jockey-less animals is Snail Racing. Events occur around the world, but the longest-standing in the UK and the one which calls itself the **World Snail Racing Championship** is held on the third Saturday in July in Congham, Norfolk.

As part of the village fête, Snail Racing has been held for forty years. The course is circular, 33cm in diameter, with the snails released in the centre. And with a shout of, 'And they're off!', the race is on. The organisers keep the course well watered during the event, especially in warmer weather, and ensure no cheating goes on; no-one sneakily throwing salt in front of a competing snail. The world record for the 33cm is held by Archie the Snail, who finished in two minutes.

The winner is presented with a trophy stuffed full of lettuce leaves.

The Shemozzle

The tiny farming town of Hunterville, in New Zealand, is home to the greatest density of Huntaway sheep and cattle dogs in the country, so it is here that they are celebrated annually in the Hunterville Huntaway Festival.

The festival has the usual fare of food, pig herding and the slightly bizarre Barking Competition, but it is the **Shemozzle** for which it is justly famous. The Shemozzle, a Yiddish-derived slang word meaning chaos and confusion, is a combination assualt course, eating competition and school sports day for a farmer and his Huntaway dog. The event, which varies in its stages every year, is a race over a distance of 2.5km for man and dog including greased slopes and vats of eels to climb through. There is also always a food element; this can be anything from having to eat dry Weetabix to sheep's eyes with cream. But after getting through all that, it's the final leg of the race which gives it uniqueness: the Huntaway jumps into a wheelbarrow, its owner picks up the handles and races the dog to the finishing line. Truly a strange game.

Calendar of Strange Events

January

Mappleton Bridge Jump – Mappleton, Ashbourne, Derbyshire. New Year's Day.
The Kirkwall Ba' Football Game – Kirkwall, Scotland. New Year's Day.
Tunarama – home of Tuna Tossing, Port Lincoln, South Australia. Last Weekend in January.
The Haxey Hood – Mob Football – Haxey, Lincolnshire. January 6.
Ponteland Wheelbarrow Races – Ponteland, North of Newcastle. New Year's Day.
Mad Maldon Mud Run – Maldon, Essex. Early January.
Annual Fruitcake Toss – Manitou Springs, Colorado, US. First Saturday in January.
Beer Barrel Chariot Racing – Llanwrtyd Wells, Wales, January.
Wolverhampton Tough Guy Race – Wolverhampton. Late January.
Krispy Kreme Challenge – Raleigh, North Carolina State University. Late January/early February.

February

The Jedburgh Hand Ba' Game – Jedburgh, Scotland. Shrove Tuesday.
The Royal Ashbourne Shrovetide Football Game – Ashbourne, Derbyshire. Shrove Tuesday.
Scoring the Hales – Alnwick, Northumberland. Shrove Tuesday.
Sedgefield Ball Game – Mob Football. Sedgefield, Co. Durham. Shrove Tuesday.
Atherstone Ball Game – Mob Football. Atherstone, Warwickshire. Shrove Tuesday.
Hurling the Silver Ball – St Ives, Cornwall. Feast Monday – the first Monday after 3 February.
Skipping Festival – Scarborough, Yorkshire. Shrove Tuesday.
UK National Indoor Tug-of-War Championships – location varies. February.
Chinchilla Melon Festival/Watermelon Ski-ing – biennial Chinchilla, Australia. February.
Glenlivet Office Putting Championship – Chicago, US. February.
Arse-Leather Sledging Championships – Neudorf, Germany. February.

March/April

Hawaiian Scottish Festival – Hawaii, April.
World Pooh Sticks Championships – Day's Lock, Oxfordshire. Last Sunday in March.
Egg Rolling – Preston, Lancashire. Easter Monday.
Clog Cobbing – Rossendale, Lancashire. Easter.
Hare Pie Scrambling and Bottle Kicking – Hallaton, Leicestershire. Easter Monday.
World Coal Carrying Championships – Gawthorpe, Yorkshire. Easter Monday.
Interstate Mullet Tossing – Florida, USA. Late April.
Snowball Fighting/Yukigassen – Kemijärvi, Finland. March/April.
Llangollen Bunny Hop – Llangollen, Wales. Easter.
Cricket Spitting/Cockroach Racing – Purdue University Bug Bowl, Indiana, USA. April.
Eel Throwing at Ely Eel Day – Ely, Cambridgeshire. Late April.
Ice Golf World Championships – Uummannaq, Greenland. March.
Spamarama – Austin, Texas. April.
Maggot Racing – Wray, Lancashire. March.

May

International Festival of Worm Charming – Blackawton, Devon. May Day Bank Holiday.
Stilton Cheese Rolling – Stilton, Cambridgeshire. May Day Bank Holiday.
Cheese Rolling – Coopers Hill, Brockworth, Gloucestershire. Spring Bank Holiday, end May.
Woolsack Racing – Tetbury, Gloucestershire. Spring Bank Holiday, end May.
Sheep Grand National – Hoo Farm, Telford, Shropshire. Early May.
Wagon Wheel Rolling – Black Horse Pub, Fulmer, Slough. May.

June

Cotswold Olimpicks, Shin Kicking – Chipping Campden, Glos. The first Friday after the second May Bank Holiday.
World Custard Pie Throwing – Maidstone, Kent. Early June.
Man versus Horse – Llanwrtyd Wells, Wales. June.
Cornish Wrestling – Royal Cornwall Show, Wadebridge, Cornwall. Early June.

World Nettle Eating Championships – Marshwood, Bridport, Dorset. Mid-June.
World Worm Charming Championships – Willaston, Cheshire. Late June/Early July.
National Sandcastle Building Competition – Woolacombe, Devon. Late June/Early July.
World Egg Throwing Championships – Thorpe Latimer, Lincolnshire. Late June.
British Town Criers Championship – Blakemere, Cheshire. June.
Watermelon Seed Spitting – Watermelon Thump, Luling, Texas, USA. Late June.
UK National Outdoor Tug-of-War Championships – Three Counties Show, Malvern, Worcestershire. Mid-June.
World Swamp Soccer Championships – Argyll, Scotland. Mid-end of June.
Goanna Pulling – Wooli, New South Wales, Aus. June.
Cartwheeling Festival – Königsallee, Düsseldorf. June.
Great Knaresborough Bed Race – Knaresborough, North Yorkshire. June.

July

Mountain Bike Bog Snorkelling – Llanwrtyd Wells, Wales. July.
World Peashooting Championships – Witcham, Cambs. July.
US Stone Skipping Championships – Mackinac Island, Northern Michigan, USA. 4 July.
The Redneck Games – East Dublin, Georgia, USA. Early July.
US Cherry Pit Spitting Championships – Eau Claire, Michigan. Early July.
World Marbles Championships – Prague, Czech Republic. July.
World Snail Racing Championships – Congham, Norfolk. July.
World Toe Wrestling Championships – Ashbourne, Derbyshire. Late July.
Dwile Flunking – Lewes Arms Pub, Lewes, Sussex. Late July.
Flounder Tramping – Palnackie, Scotland. Mid-July.
Winkle Spitting – Mogueric, Brittany, France. Mid July.
Conger Cuddling – Lyme Regis, Dorset. July.
Rolling Pin and Brick Throwing – Stroud, Gloucestershire, Canada, USA. July.
Wife Carrying Championships – Sonkajärvi, Finland. Early July.
The Stanga Games/Gotlandic Olympics – Gotland, Sweden. July.
Darwin Beer Can Regatta – Darwin, NT, Australia. July.
UK Mobile Phone Throwing – Battersea Park, London. July.
Pillow Fighting World Championships – Kenwood, California. 4 July.

August

Brambles Cricket Match – Isle of Wight. August.
Kubb World Championships – Gotland, Sweden. Early August.
Totnes Orange Roll – Totnes, Devon. August.
River Football – Bourton-on-the-Water, Gloucestershire. August Bank Holiday.
Bog Snorkelling – Llanwrtyd Wells, Wales. August Bank Holiday.
La Giostra del Maialetto – Segni, Lazio, Italy. First 2 weeks of August.
International Bathtub Regatta – Dinant, Belgium. August.
National Canal Jumping Contest – Netherlands. August.
World Mobile Phone Throwing Contest – Savonlinna, Finland. Last week of August.
Potato Days Festival/Potato Wrestling – Barnesville, Minnesota. Late August.
Wales Open Stone Skimming Championships – Castle Pond, Pembroke. August.
Wisconsin State Cow Chip Throw – Prairie du Sac, Wisconsin. Labour Day Weekend (end August/early September).
World Sauna Championships – Heinola, Finland. August.
Krevzberg versus Friedrichshain Food Fight – August.

September

Bognor Birdman – Bognor Regis, Sussex. September.
British Minigolf Championships – location varies. Mid-September.
Pewsey Wheelbeero Race – Pewsey, Wiltshire. Mid-September.
World Stone Skimming Championships – Easdale Island, Argyll, Scotland. Late September.
Winton Outback Festival – Winton, Queensland, Aus. Last week in September.
World Black Pudding Throwing Championships – Ramsbottom, Lancashire. September.
World Gurning Championships – Egremont, West Cumbria. September.
Egremont Crab Fair – Egremont, Cumbria. September.
World Gravy Wrestling – Pennine Festival of Food, Darwen, Lancashire. September.

October

World Rock Paper Scissors Championships – location varies. Mid-October.

Nova Scotia Pumpkin Regatta – Windsor, Nova Scotia. October.
World Conker Championships – Ashton, Northamptonshire. Second Sunday in October.
Irish Conker Championship – Freshford, Co. Kilkenny. End of October.
Sherston Scrump: Mangold Hurling – Sherston, Wiltshire. October.
World Pea Throwing Championships – Lewes Arms Pub, Lewes, Sussex. October.
Hunterville Huntaway Festival/The Shemozzle – Hunterville, Australia. Late October.
High-heel Racing – Washington DC, USA. October.
World Crazy Golf Championships – Hastings, East Sussex. October.

November

Barrel Racing – Ottery St Mary, Devon. 5 November.

December

The Kirkwall Ba' Football Game – Kirkwall, Scotland. Christmas Day.
The Great Christmas Pudding Race – Covent Garden, London. Early December.

Internet Resources

Strange Games – the blog   www.strange-games.blogspot.com

Hand and Feet Games
Bloody Knuckles Association   www.bloodyknuckles.net
World Rock Paper Scissors Society   www.rpschamps.com
Rock Paper Scissors 101   www.umop.com/rps101.htm
Bob 'the Rock' Cooper –   www.backbob.com
Britain's RPS World Champion
World Finger Jousting Federation   www.fingerjoust.com
Universal Pen Spinning Board   www.upsb.info
Shin Kicking Association of Britain   www.daeschner.com/skab
Cotswold Olimpick Games   www.olimpickgames.co.uk
Slapsies (computer game)   www.flash-x-games.com/
game/operation_slaps.shtml

House Gymnastics   www.housegymnastics.com
Paper Football Association   www.paperfootball.us
Wallhooky Resource Page   www.wallhooky.com
UK Tug-of-War Association   www.tugofwar.co.uk
Ashton Conker Club   www.worldconkerchampionships.com
Fédération Française de Conkers   www.ffconkers.org

Outdoor Games
Extreme Ironing   www.extremeironing.com
Extreme Poker   www.interpoker.com/tournaments/
extreme_poker.shtml

Kubb World Championship   www.vmkubb.com

Urban Games

Street Wars	www.streetwars.net
Pac Manhattan – Urban Pacman	www.pacmanhattan.com

Festivals

Ottery St Mary Tar Barrels	www.otterytarbarrels.co.uk
Spamarama	www.spamarama.org
International Bognor Birdman	www.birdman.org.uk
World Bog Snorkelling	www.worldbogsnork.com
Welsh Bog Snorkelling	www.green-events.co.uk/ eventinfo.php?eventdetails=54
Australian Bog Snorkelling	www.bogsnorkeling.com
Winton Outback Festival – Home to the Dunny Derby	www.outbackfestival.org
Conconully Outhouse Races	www.conconully.com/outhouse.htm
World Gurning at Egremont Crab Fair	www.egremontcrabfair.org.uk
The Bottle Inn – Home of Nettle Eating	www.thebottleinn.co.uk
Potato Days Festival	www.potatodays.com
The Redneck Games	www.summerredneckgames.com
Showa-Shinzan International Yukigassen, Japan	www.yukigassen.jp/ english/index.html
Finnish Yukigassen – Snowball Festival	www.yukigassenfi.aazilla.com/
Wolverhampton Tough Guy Race	www.toughguy.co.uk
World Worm Charming Championships	www.wormcharming.com

Throwing and Propulsion Games

Official Cherry Pit Spitting Handbook	www.treemendus-fruit.com/ pit-spit_handbook.htm
Watermelon Thumping	www.watermelonthump.com
Beaver Cow Chip News	www.bvrcowchipnews.com/ cowchip_news.htm
Wisconsin State Cow Chip Throw	www.wiscowchip.com

World Egg Throwing Federation	www.swatonvintageday.ssl powered.com/index.html
World Haggis Hurling	www.scottishhaggis.co.uk/ haggis_hurling.htm
UK Mangold Hurling Association	www.mangoldhurling.co.uk
Mobile Phone Throwing WC	www.savonlinnafestivals.com
UK Mobile Phone Throwing	www.mobilephonethrowing.co.uk
Lewes Arms Pub – Home of World Pea Throwing Championships	www.lewesarms.org.uk
World Stone Skimming Championships	www.stoneskimming.com
Wales Open Stone Skimming	www.skimwales.com
North American Stone Skipping Association (NASSA)	www.yeeha.net/nassa/a1.html
Tunarama – Tuna Tossing Festival	www.tunarama.net
US Interstate Mullet Throwing	www.florabama.com/Special Events/MulletToss/ mullet_toss_faq.htm
World Pea Shooting Championships	www.witcham.org.uk/_sgg/ m1m6_1.htm

Sports

US Bicycle Polo Association, Inc.	www.bikepolo.com
Finnish Swamp Soccer	www.suopotkupallo.fi
UK Swamp Soccer	www.swampsoccer.co.uk
Splashdiving	www.splashdiving.com
Stilton Cheese Rolling	www.stilton.org
Gloucestershire Cheese Rolling	www.cheese-rolling.co.uk
World Chess Boxing Organisation	www.wcbo.org
Krispy Kreme Challenge	www.krispykremechallenge.com
Hanetball	www.hanetball.com
Mad Maldon Mud Run	www.maldonmudrace.com

The Ba' Game	www.bagame.com
The Haxey Hood	www.wheewall.com/hood/
British Pedal Car Racing	www.pedalcars.info
Chinchilla Melon Festival	www.melonfest.com.au
(Watermelon Ski-ing)	
Ponteland Wheelbarrow Races	www.pontelandonline.co.uk/ html/wheelbarrow_race.html
Tetbury Woolsack Racing	www.tetburywoolsack.co.uk
World Coal Carrying Championships	www.gawthorpe.ndo.co.uk/coal.htm
British Minigolf Association	www.minigolf.org.uk/joomla
World Crazy Golf Championships	www.miniaturegolfer.com/ world_crazy_golf_championships.html
World Office Putting Championships	www.cigarlife.com/eventz /glen_putt_champs.htm
World Ice Golf Championships	www.greenland-guide.gl/icegolf
World Pooh Sticks Championships	www.pooh-sticks.com

Animal Games

Hunterville Shemozzle	www.shemozzle.co.nz

Index